Timeless
Running Wisdom

Richard Benyo

Human Kinetics

Library of Congress Cataloging-in-Publication Data

Benyo, Richard.
  Timeless running wisdom / Richard Benyo.
      p. cm.
  Includes bibliographical references.
  ISBN-13: 978-0-7360-9934-9 (soft cover)
  ISBN-10: 0-7360-9934-4 (soft cover)
  1. Running--Anecdotes. 2. Running--Training--Anecdotes. I. Title.
  GV1061.B446 2010
  796.42--dc22

                                    2010036497

ISBN-10: 0-7360-9934-4 (print)
ISBN-13: 978-0-7360-9934-9 (print)

The Web addresses cited in this text were current as of September 2010, unless otherwise noted.

Acquisitions Editor: Laurel Plotzke Garcia; **Developmental Editor:** Anne Hall; **Assistant Editors:** Elizabeth Evans and Tyler Wolpert; **Copyeditor:** Patsy Fortney; **Graphic Designer:** Fred Starbird; **Graphic Artist:** Kim McFarland; **Cover Designer:** Keith Blomberg; **Photographer (cover):** ASICS America; **Photographer (interior):** © Human Kinetics, unless otherwise noted; **Photo Asset Manager:** Laura Fitch; **Photo Production Manager:** Jason Allen; **Printer:** Sheridan Press

Human Kinetics books are available at special discounts for bulk purchase. Special editions or book excerpts can also be created to specification. For details, contact the Special Sales Manager at Human Kinetics.

Printed in the United States of America   10 9 8 7 6 5 4 3 2 1

The paper in this book is certified under a sustainable forestry program.

Human Kinetics
Web site: www.HumanKinetics.com

United States: Human Kinetics
P.O. Box 5076
Champaign, IL 61825-5076
800-747-4457
e-mail: humank@hkusa.com

Canada: Human Kinetics
475 Devonshire Road Unit 100
Windsor, ON N8Y 2L5
800-465-7301 (in Canada only)
e-mail: info@hkcanada.com

Europe: Human Kinetics
107 Bradford Road
Stanningley
Leeds LS28 6AT, United Kingdom
+44 (0) 113 255 5665
e-mail: hk@hkeurope.com

Australia: Human Kinetics
57A Price Avenue
Lower Mitcham, South Australia 5062
08 8372 0999
e-mail: info@hkaustralia.com

New Zealand: Human Kinetics
P.O. Box 80
Torrens Park, South Australia 5062
0800 222 062
e-mail: info@hknewzealand.com

E524

This one's for all the long-running friends encountered along the roads and trails, so many of whom served as a welcome aid station in the midst of the human race.

Contents

Foreword

This book and a pair of running shoes just may be the only two things you need as a runner. Rich Benyo is the author of the most reputable running- and fitness-related publications, and he has done it again. In *Timeless Running Wisdom* he documents miles of running revelations so you don't have to reinvent that painful wheel. The result of his many experiences is a faster, stronger, and smarter athlete. In fact, he was fast enough to chase down the greatest runners of his acquaintance, such as Bill Rodgers, Kathrine Switzer, Dean Karnazes, and my hero, Joan Benoit-Samuelson, all of whom contributed to this book. They are paving a smoother road for you, pointing out and even removing the roots and rocks on your favorite trails so you can glide along, chasing your next runner's high. You hold in your hands the best compilation of running strategy and advice available.

Distance running has a way of unveiling the depths of our character and in the process teaches us how to pursue our wildest dreams. It isn't until we are deep into a run that we find our groove and tap into our smarter, more profound selves. It takes some mileage under our fluid belt to experience these ah-ha! moments. This book is a collection of those moments from people who have logged enough miles to have figured it all out the hard way. The wisdom of this book comes from many miles of experience from the most pivotal stars this sport has ever known. You hold in your hands, bound between covers, stories of the emotional highs, hapless pitfalls, and stunning awareness that running offers.

From a sport that seems as simple as putting one foot in front of the other comes a wide spectrum of advice and stories from those who have repeatedly gone the distance.

Runners will relate to and learn from this book, but you don't need to be a runner to take from it the full experience of people who have challenged themselves and triumphed in their own special ways. The secrets of their successes are now in your hands. And whether "running" to you means competing in a race, running errands, or running a business, you will gain enough wisdom to make the journey a winning one.

Rich Benyo and his long-running running friends make up my Running Fantasy Camp. *Timeless Running Wisdom* presents what is truly the Dream Team of running's most notable athletes and personalities. They own the shoes we'd love to fill, and we are honored that they are more than willing to help us get a perfect fit.

Consider chapter 1 your first day of spring training. In some instances the stars of the sport did it wrong the first time and learned from their

mistakes, allowing you to skip over the rough parts in the road. Or maybe you've already tried it yourself and had less-than-sterling results; it is uplifting to know that the heroes and heroines of the sport have been there, have made similar mistakes, and yet picked themselves up and prospered. This is your chance to learn from the wise without puking on a nearby runner, suffering the horrid pain of bleeding nipples while wearing a brand-new white racing singlet, or climbing out of a run that has the potential to be a six-foot hole. With this book you can access all the knowledge and suffer none of the pain.

Identify and learn your lessons from the comfort of your favorite recliner. You know the one I mean: the one that seems to have a magnet in it tuned to your body in the wake of a long midsummer run. Yeah, that's right. The one festooned with energy bar wrappers shoved behind the cushions and bagel crumbs that stick to the backs of your legs when you are finally able to pry yourself up. That chair. Your favorite. Combined with your new favorite running book.

You are about to read your way to a better running experience, and in the process you won't even get winded. Your most successful self is waiting within you to be released, and the chapters of this book may very well be the keys you are seeking. You will be both enlightened and entertained by the experiences shared by this all-star collection of running legends.

Let *Timeless Running Wisdom* be your coach and your training partner, the best mentor you can possibly find. Read it. Put it away safely on a shelf. Then read it again when your running needs a fresh approach or you need to adapt. There are stories in this book for every runner, *beginner or veteran,* something identifiable and true.

Deena Kastor

Introduction

If wisdom automatically came with age, there would be no such thing as an old fool.

Someone who's been around a long time often learns little from the aging process and the passage through decades of experience, but instead becomes simply more of what he or she always was, whether stubborn as a mule or sweet as maple syrup. Nevertheless, by observing and taking part in a certain activity for an enormous amount of time, specific, immutable truths become self-evident. Often, those self-evident truths come to us the hard way—from doing something the wrong way often enough that the obvious eventually dawns on us: This isn't working; there must be a better way to do this.

If we are lucky, a mentor full of wisdom and generosity takes us in tow and proceeds to head us off from going down yet another blind alley. We learn also—again, often after some time—that no matter how much the activity is changed from the outside, inside it is as it always was. It may be festooned with bells and whistles, but underneath it is still the same.

When we jettison the irrelevant complexities too often attached to running, what remains is the simple sweetness of the sport, the joy of natural movement, and the rich lifestyle that accompanies it. "Sweet running" occurs when the elements of training and effort intersect and the training has been just slightly more ambitious than you had planned. The effort becomes, for a moment or for an hour, "effortless." The myriad of training levels involved in running—-physical, mental, spiritual—-blend in a seemingly cosmic recipe, and we are one with the run.

The Irish poet W.B. Yeats asked, "How can we know the dancer from the dance?" So, too, the runner runs. For that period in time, a person is uniquely both the subject and the predicate—one and the same, both at once, the beginning and the middle of a sentence.

When does this intersection happen? It can begin as early as two months into a running program, when the heart and lungs have become running-fit and the appendages and major organs are coming into their own. But more commonly, it appears when all body systems are equally fit and flowing together.

Over the years, running pundits have referred to the sensation as "the runner's high." Elite runners, however, especially of the long-distance variety, have pooh-poohed it. William Glasser, MD, wrote a book about this subject in the mid-1970s titled *Positive Addiction*. He contended

that long-distance runners can sustain such a seemingly boring activity because they become addicted to the rhythm of the activity, that a runner's high is possible when a runner who is in good condition runs well in an uncritical way. Glasser contended that elite runners do not experience runner's highs because they run too self-critically, measuring their breaths and monitoring the current condition of their legs. They are more like highly technical space shuttles than red tail hawks joyously swimming along a river of wind.

John Jerome speaks of "the sweet spot in time" as it applies to sport in his 1980 book of the same title. Speaking of throwing rocks at bottles lined up on a riverbank, John speaks of the increasing efficiency he experienced as his arm warmed up and his eyes became better at estimating the distance. "Mostly I recall the haunting power I felt on the occasional throw when I knew as the stone left my hand that it was going to hit its target"(p. 14).

Some would refer to that experience as peak performance, but it's not. Peak performance is much rarer than hitting that sweet spot in time.

When the famed late mythologist Joseph Campbell was interviewed by Bill Moyers on the classic PBS series *The Power of Myth*, the subject of peak performance came up. Moyers asked Campbell if he'd ever enjoyed a peak experience. My wife and I were at the time watching the series with a group of Palo Alto intellectuals who were stalwart fans of Campbell. When Moyers posed the question, several of the group perked up, certain that Joseph Campbell would cite a moment while taking part in a Malaysian tribal ceremony or riding the ropes that connected to the bells in the cathedral of Chartres or while reading a good book. He disappointed them. Instead of describing some exotic ritual, Campbell cited two peak experiences—both of them somewhat exotic to the sedentary lifestyle of the Stanfordites in attendance. His two peak experiences came when he ran the anchor leg during two different races for his Columbia University track relay team; when he accepted the baton on those final laps, he knew that there was no human being in the world who would catch him.

Was it sweet running in both of those instances? Yes, it was. But Campbell undoubtedly had other periods of sweet running. Peak experiences are rare; sweet spots, especially in running, are not necessarily so rare. In fact, they can be fairly common, if we learn to bring together all the critical—but not critiqued—elements and to ride them in an uncritical way.

Dr. Mihaly Csikszentmihalyi is a professor and former chairman of the Department of Psychology at the University of Chicago. He has spent decades studying this phenomenon on the broader scale in life; in his studies and his writing, he refers to it as "flow."

"The best moments usually occur," Professor Csikszentmihalyi contends in *Flow: The Psychology of Optimal Experience*, "when a person's body or mind is stretched to its limits in a voluntary effort to accomplish something difficult and worthwhile. Optimal experience is thus something that we *make* happen" (1991, p. 3).

"Optimal experience," then, does not come to those who sit and wait. Like the sweet spot or the runner's high, or peak performance or sweet running, or just plain running wisdom, we must actively seek it—or at least prepare for it actively on a physical level. We must eschew the sedentary notion, or as running guru Dr. George Sheehan frequently used to say, "Never trust an idea that comes to you while you're sitting down."

Many runners experience sweet running on their own. Any runner who has trained vigorously and wisely for a marathon and who leaves the starting line conservatively usually experiences a sweet spot between miles 7 and 16, once the deep muscles are warmed up and the rhythm of running has established itself, and before the weariness of running a very long distance arrives. But many a marathoner has lost a marathon during that period of sweet running by mistakenly assuming that he or she somehow magically trained beyond the perfect level, only to proceed to outrun his or her fine-tuning in a greedy effort to take advantage of prowess that, at least that day, is not present in such abundance.

This book is not about training to run, but rather, about running to train yourself to get more sweetness from your running, from exacting more wisdom by squeezing from running what is simplest and best. This book does not describe what training to do as much as it discusses how to do it in all its forms, from running fast to resting, from learning the historical footsteps in which you run to experiencing the joys of running wild and alone—while, as often as possible, licking and then savoring the sweetness from it. Hopefully, this will spare you the chore of laboring too many years to gain wisdom, when on some levels it is self-evident and available to those eager to embrace it.

Too many runners, especially those new to the sport or lifestyle, spend way too much time and energy asking this question: Am I doing this right? This tendency is especially overpowering for new runners who do have a background in sport. Is there a right and wrong way to run? Of course, but there are as many right ways of doing it as there are runners.

Stand at the finish line of a road race and watch the runners approach. Does every runner exhibit exactly the same running style? No way. Some are human examples of poetry in motion. Some tend to flail and waste a lot of sideways motion. But does the runner with the classic style always beat the runner with the flailing arms? Certainly not. Watch a film of the late great Czech runner Emil Zatopek, who won the 5,000 meters, 10,000 meters, and the marathon in the 1952

Helsinki Olympic Games. His running style has been described as that of a "man recently stabbed through the heart" (Sandrock, *Running,* p. 3). But another observer cautioned track experts not to pay attention to what was happening with Emil's upper body, but rather to observe what was happening from the waist down. To date, no other runner has accomplished the Olympic long-distance "triple" that Emil did, and probably no runner ever will.

If you've checked out the table of contents, you may have noticed pairs of chapters that seem to contradict each other—such as Run With a Plan (chapter 9) and Run by Feel (chapter 10), and Run Alone (chapter 17) and Run Together (chapter 18). I've done this for runners who have been at it for quite a while; often, what works perfectly well one year may contain the kiss of death for a running program the next year.

This book refrains from overglorifying the marathon, which has grown to become the holy grail of long-distance runners. Jesse Owens never ran a marathon, and he was a "real runner." You don't need to run a marathon to be considered a real runner, although training like a marathoner will greatly enhance your pathway to sweet running and the attendant wisdom—no matter what the distance.

If I'd wanted to push the marathon, I'd have titled the book *Timeless Marathon Wisdom.* Besides, the marathon doesn't need a push from me. In fact, it might be good if the marathon were given less emphasis, so that we'd have fewer runners who get into the sport and immediately, without putting in their time and without learning to run shorter distances, take on the marathon and fall out the other side injured or burned out—or both.

Like the human body itself, which becomes more efficient the more you use it, running becomes sweeter the more you integrate it into your life. The wisdom comes from allowing that to happen. Relax in your running and allow your own wisdom to sweeten the whole process.

Before we get to the body of this book, let me give you 10 bits of running wisdom that some of us learned through trial and error (mostly error):

1. ***Did it this way:*** To reward myself for putting in 18 weeks of hard training toward a marathon, I bought myself a brand-new running outfit so for once I'd look color-coordinated in my finisher picture.

   Result: Chafed and bloody inner thighs and a grimace on my face in my finisher picture.

   Wisdom: Never, ever wear or use anything in a race that you haven't broken in during practice runs.

2. **Did it this way:** I thought I could run through a sore calf muscle if I warmed up sufficiently first.

   Result: My calf got worse, and by overcompensating for that pain, I developed an additional injury on the opposite side of my body.

   Wisdom: When injured, cut back or stop running entirely. Or, train in a different environment that does not aggravate the injury, such as running in a pool.

3. **Did it this way:** Not wanting to have a race number flapping against my chest, I pinned it to my shorts.

   Result: Paper cuts on my right thigh.

   Wisdom: Take a look at the professional runners. Where do they put their bib numbers? At the middle of their chests, of course.

4. **Did it this way:** Wanting to ensure that I'd have enough carbohydrates on board, I ate a hearty breakfast before a long run.

   Results: First, I felt like a slug; second, I fertilized a farmer's field by throwing the hearty breakfast back up so that I ultimately had no reserves of carbs.

   Wisdom: If you want something in your stomach before you go out on a long run, eat something bland (a bagel, for instance) long enough before your workout or race so that it will have been absorbed by your body so your stomach doesn't divert blood from the working muscles.

5. **Did it this way:** I thought that if one long run on a weekend was good, two of them would be twice as good.

   Result: The following two weeks were pitiful as I dealt with legs that didn't want to move.

   Wisdom: Alternate between hard and easy runs so that your body can adequately recover from the harder or longer workouts.

6. **Did it this way:** I ran all seven days of the week.

   Result: Weariness and heavy legs.

   Wisdom: Rest days are recovery days that lead to higher-quality training days down the calendar.

7. **Did it this way:** I started out fast to put some time in the bank.

   Result: The final miles had no sparkle to them; in fact, they were a downward spiral.

   Wisdom: You can't cash in on time put in the bank if it hasn't had time to mature.

8. **Did it this way:** I went into the marathon with too little training.

   Result: I used the final six miles to offer penance for all the sins I'd committed in the first 10 years of my life.

   Wisdom: You reap what you sow. Sow too little and reap a lot . . . of pain.

9. **Did it this way:** I didn't hydrate because I believed that only weenies drink fluids before and during a race.

   Results: Dehydration, desiccation, and DNF (did not finish).

   Wisdom: Stay hydrated before, during, and after a race, but don't overdo it. Learn how much hydration is just enough for you.

10. **Did it this way:** After crossing the finish line at a marathon, I saw a nice patch of grass and dropped onto it.

    Result: My legs felt like someone had poured concrete down them. I needed help to get up and limped away like a rusted robot.

    Wisdom: When you cross the finish line of a race, keep moving to pump some of the waste out of your legs; after the race, walk at least a quarter-mile for each five miles raced. You'll come back surprisingly well over the next several days.

    And, of course, the obvious admonition: Do as I say, not as I did.

Because, even after all of these decades, my wisdom in running is limited, I prevailed on some of my long-running running buddies to share some of their hard-won wisdom. Enormous thanks to this all-star team!

Here's a thumbnail on each of those long-running friends, which isn't all that easy to do because an entire book could be written on each of them.

Kathrine Switzer is best-known for entering the 1967 Boston Marathon as "K.V. Switzer" with no intent to defraud, but rather to be part of her Syracuse team, then being assaulted by Jock Semple, a race official; but she is more famed to many of us as the gal who worked tirelessly behind the scenes to get the women's marathon into the Olympic Games. Oh, yes, and she's a terrific writer.

Amby Burfoot is one of the sages of long-distance running. Winner of the 1968 Boston Marathon, we were fortunate enough to hire him as the East Coast Editor of *Runner's World* back in 1978, and he's been a stalwart of that magazine ever since. Amby is one of the nicest guys you'll ever meet, and a mighty fine scribe.

Joe Henderson was the first full-time editor of *Runner's World* when Bob Anderson moved the magazine from Kansas to Northern California

in 1970. I got to work with Joe at *Runner's World* when I took over his editorship in 1977, and had even more fun than a writer is supposed to have when we collaborated on *The Running Encyclopedia*. Such collaborations often result in feuds, but the experience brought us closer than ever.

Hal Higdon and I used to cover auto sports back in the 1970s; he's the author of some mighty fine auto racing books, including *Showdown at Daytona*. He knew I'd run in college and when Joe Henderson's position at *Runner's World* was opening up, he twisted Bob Anderson's arm to get me the job. But I still like him anyway.

Dick Beardsley personifies the word "indomitable." In the wake of emerging as one of America's premier marathoners, he went through some of the most disastrous accidents anybody could imagine, but he emerged from every one of them filled with enthusiasm and high spirits. He set the course record at the Napa Valley Marathon, where I'm chairman of the board, and we love to have him come back and visit every March.

Mel Williams is the definition of the Renaissance man: an accomplished academic, age-group winner at places like the Boston Marathon, world-traveler, and friend to everyone he meets. He is also one of the spark-plugs of the running world in and around Norfolk.

Joan Benoit-Samuelson is to most runners the personification of a gritty, hard-working runner, gloriously triumphant at the first-ever women's Olympic marathon in 1984. I'll never forget the first time I met her, way back in 1979, when she won the *Runner's World* Nurmi Award as the best U.S. female runner and arrived wearing a sensible Maine sweater and becoming emotional over her award. She is one of the sweetest people in running, until she pins on a race number.

Dean Karnazes has probably done more to get people thinking in terms of doing outrageous running challenges than anyone else on the planet. He is constantly thinking up challenges to which he can apply his considerable talents, like running 50 marathons in 50 states in 50 days. He's a marvelous spokesman for the sport of ultrarunning, which is a world out there in the outer limits where the air is rare.

Lorraine Moller was perhaps the most dominating female marathoners of her era, winning an outrageous percentage of the marathons she entered. She won three of the Avon International Marathons while no other woman won more than one. She won numerous times at Grandma's Marathon and at Osaka Ladies' Marathon. Her recent autobiography, *On the Wings of Mercury*, is a must-read.

Marshall Ulrich never met a challenge that he didn't like. Besides racking up more miles than any other human being on the treacherous Death Valley course, he ran across the U.S. in 2008 (while injured) and climbed to the summit of the highest peak on all seven continents. Yet to his friends, he's just plain ole "Marsh."

"Boston Billy" Rodgers probably did more to get American baby boomers out of their easy chairs and onto the roads than anyone else before or since. An affable guy-next-door kind of fellow, Billy made winning races look easy in the late 1970s and early 1980s. He won Boston and New York four times each, and was famous for remembering virtually any running statistic there was but forgetting where he'd parked his car.

Allan Steinfeld has long been one of the quiet "movers" of the sport. Allan worked with Fred Lebow to grow the New York City Marathon to the pinnacle of big-city marathons. He took over from Fred when Fred was diagnosed with brain cancer, and carried the marathon to new heights. Self-effacing and modest, Allan was present behind the scenes for nearly every significant running advancement over the past three decades.

Roger Robinson has long been a triple-threat: accomplished academic (his lectures at Victoria University in Wellington, NZ were constantly oversubscribed), his writing on running has been a staple in the running world for decades, and he had a reign as one of the best masters marathoners in the world, winning Boston and New York and at one point going unbeaten as a masters runner in more than 100 races in a row.

It has been an honor to work with such a wonderful team of friends on this project.

Most of these running relationships go back decades and have grown more precious and dear as the years have marched on by us, leaving most of these folks unscathed—except for the occasional ache or pain, and the inevitability of hair turning grayer, making them appear even more mature . . . and therefore, wiser.

It's with great humility that I thank them for their generosity in coming forth and saving my sorry ass from looking like a know-it-all who doesn't.

Wisdom: Run long enough and often enough and you accumulate a wonderful array of friends.

Rich Benyo
Sonoma County, California

Chris Mautz/fotolia.com

EMBRACE SIMPLICITY

A few days ago, I beheld a truly wondrous sight. I was lumbering (which is my form of off-season jogging, complete with long pants and the sartorial appearance of the homeless) down a paved bike and pedestrian path near our home. Coming toward me was what appeared to be a cut-rate cosmonaut.

He was a mid-20s fella lumbering no faster than I was, and I'm pushing three times his age. The poor lout was burdened by more than a mule's load of equipment. He wore a heart-rate monitor strapped around his chest with the receiver on one wrist; a wrist-mounted GPS thing-am-a-jig on the other wrist; a hydration system strapped to his back; a portable CD player with headphones, the player strapped to his left upper arm; a pair of high-tech computerized running shoes; a Batman-like utility belt loaded with GU packets and other stuff I did not recognize; and to complete the ensemble, ankle weights.

I sent out sensors to determine whether the ground under him was quaking. We do, after all, have frequent quakes here in Northern California. As we passed each other, I said, "Hey! How's it goin'? Nice day, huh?"

He said nothing, acknowledged nothing, moved forward like one of those automated vacuum cleaners you see advertised on cable channels at night that won't change direction until they bump into something. I literally stopped in my tracks and watched him slowly trundle away.

What, I asked myself, has become of running as the oldest, simplest sport in the history of humankind, the sport that started with the ultimate prize: life itself? You outrun the saber-toothed tiger, and you live. You don't outrun the saber-toothed tiger, and you are removed from the gene pool in favor of someone who can. You run down the antelope by wearing it out, and you and your tribe eat and live one more week. You fail to run down the antelope, and you and your tribe die out in favor of a tribe that can consistently run down the antelope.

In our modern world where saber-toothed tigers come skeletonized in museums of natural history, we pay people to capture and butcher and sometimes even serve up the antelope with a garlic-and-caper gravy. We take home medals to prove that we entered and completed the race and are quite the fellow or gal, and all is well with the world. Now, let's eat!

After the burdened man disappeared, I looked down at myself and felt diminished, out of it, retro. Given that it was early December, I wore a pair of briefs covered by a pair of tan rugged slacks, an old sweatshirt, a pair of socks, and a pair of well-broken-in running shoes. I did wear a digital watch, but the chronograph feature wasn't engaged. I was out for a run: to hear the birds chirp, to smell the dog crap that self-righteous dog lovers had "forgotten" to clean up, to check out how high the creek had risen after the last rain.

I started running again, shuffling along, puzzled enough by the question of whether the guy I'd just passed was enjoying himself that I felt compelled to haul down from the mental archives the exact moment running had gone from the simplest, cheapest sport in the world to one of the most technical. I asked myself whether we had gained anything in performance when we made the devil's deal to have technology dominate our runs.

The topic had come up a few weeks earlier as I worked on an issue of *Marathon & Beyond*. The little bimonthly carries a column each issue called "On the Mark," wherein a reader sends in a question and I send it out to a handful of experts, who answer it in their own unique ways. On occasion, I pretend to be an expert and answer the question myself.

This was one of those occasions. The question was from a young woman who had yet to run a marathon and who trained with a guy who purchased every technical toy that hit the market. Jayne Doddard concluded her question with this observation: "I swear that one of the reasons my friend doesn't run faster than he does is he spends so much time and energy consulting his 'stuff.'"

I concluded that Jayne already knew the answer, but she had hooked me with her question, so I jumped right in:

> It sometimes takes an enormous stretch of the credible to encompass the beautiful simplicity of running and the complex technological morass it can become.
>
> In the mid-'60s, when I ran college cross-country, the biggest technological innovation was that we got to train and race in lighter-than-walking-around training flats. Our team practiced in red cotton shorts and plain gray T-shirts. Our meets were timed with a manually wound stopwatch, and our coach timed our workouts with his high-tech wristwatch—high-tech because it was a 'self-winding' watch that was kept wound by the fact that the front end of his '62 Rambler was out of whack from his summer trips to Bogotá, Colombia, to brush up on his Spanish, so the vibrating steering wheel kept his watch wound tighter than Ringo Starr's drumhead.
>
> We ran pretty well in those years. Good enough to place second in the Pennsylvania State College cross-country championship meet in the fall of '64.
>
> In the late '70s and early '80s, while I worked at *Runner's World*, there were innovations galore. Every week the mailman brought packages of everything from Bone Fones (a radio device that you

slung over your shoulders and that played music for you while you ran by sending vibrations through your collarbones) to the Genesis Biometrics pulse monitor (*RW*, November 1980, p. 94: 'Only Genesis—monitors pulse rate—computes exercise time within your specified zone—measures recovery time to base pulse rate—provides audible alert system—paces rhythm with adjustable metronome—tells time in hours and minutes.' And if you ordered it off the ad on page 94, you got a pair of running shoes free.), which was larger than Dick Tracy's wrist-radio and had a wire connecting it to a gadget you slipped over your finger so it could monitor your pulse. The only problem was that if you moved, it didn't register anything; you had to stand still for it to slowly compute your pulse.

None of the stuff made us run any better. Running better came from . . . running harder and smarter.

Come to think of it, there was one electronic device that made us run better in the '80s. It was a wrist chronograph that provided an audible beep to dictate the wearer's running rhythm; if someone near us in a race was wearing one of those damned things, we were motivated to run faster to get away from the infernal beeping."

And so the answer (or rant) went.

I thought now about turning around and running after the weigheddown runner to ask him a question: Why? I couldn't imagine that he was enjoying his running any more than he enjoyed staying late after work to take on a few extra projects the boss had hitched to his annual review.

At the occasional running seminar, I've been known to refer to longdistance runners as aerobic astronauts, but this guy trumped even them. The poor guy was prepared to go into deep space without missing a beat. Actually, he'd never miss a beat because it looked as though every one was counted.

Running and other aerobic sports are touted as stress relievers, and technically, they are—if we let them work naturally without strapping on more technical junk than tinsel on a Christmas tree.

Let's face it: Some stress is good. Without physical stress, we'd all turn into jellied blobs—just like sedentary people do. To function, a muscle must be stressed on a regular basis. Opposing muscles must be stressed or else the muscle pushing or pulling in one direction will overpower its opposite muscle.

But more psychological stress we don't need. We certainly don't need to go out and pay good money to add more stress by accessorizing our-

selves with gadgets that measure our every bodily function. We can get all the stress we want free of charge.

You'll recall Yeats' quote in the introduction with the corollary that we cannot separate the runner from the run. Of course, this is true only if we are careful not to burden what happens naturally with technological flotsam and jetsam.

How can daily running slip into sweet running if we are burdened like mules? Hell, even a mule wouldn't stand for that kind of overload abuse. I do occasionally run across mules along the pedestrian path I was traipsing that day. Sometimes I stop and converse with them; they may be stubborn, but they ain't dumb. Every time I see them, I think of the old mule skinner axiom: The dumbest mule is smarter than the smartest horse. A horse will keep running until it dies. A mule will stand its ground and say, "Hey, man. Screw you. I ain't movin' until you remove some of this crap from my back."

Perhaps we can forge a new axiom: The dumbest mule is smarter than the smartest horse, and the dumbest horse is smarter than the smartest techie runner.

Sounds plausible.

Does high-tech running produce enormous benefits? Chapter 2 presents some prime statistics that prove that it does not. An enormous amount of technical crap has been invented and marketed over the past 20 years, and the average marathon time in the United States has slowed by more than an hour.

If we want to experience better running, sweet running, we need sweet music to accompany our running. And the sweetest music is the rhythmic sound of our lungs drawing in oxygen and expelling carbon dioxide. It is the rhythm of life itself. Even against a backdrop of honking car horns and steady white noise, the sound of rhythmic breathing asserts itself as the dominant beat. Throw in a bird chirp as a counterpoint, and it doesn't get much better.

Do we need to measure our every heartbeat while on a run? Certainly, heart-rate monitors have their place. They're especially useful for holding us back on scheduled easy running days so our bodies can repair themselves, thereby increasing efficiency. They are also good for holding us back in the early portions of a race, although the anxiety of the race situation often results in false readings of our readiness to run harder than usual.

Do we need high-tech everything to run, or are we merely extending the overload of our daily lives to our running because we need to be connected to an electronic teat?

How much stuff do world-class ballet dancers strap to themselves? If it were culturally permissible, I suspect they might want to shed some of the confining garments they do wear so their dancing would be even

more natural. They might dance nude, the same way the ancient Greeks competed in the ancient Olympics.

I am not advocating for runners to run nude (although several road races encourage a state of undress), but nude does have its place. Mark Remy, the daily blogger at *Runner's World*, wrote a humorous book titled *The Runner's Rule Book: Everything a Runner Needs to Know—And Then Some*. On page 47, he explains rule 1.44: One Day a Week, Run Naked. What does he mean by that? "Once a week—maybe on an easy day—leave your running watch at home, head out the door, and just . . . run. While you're at it, leave your GPS at home, too, and your heart-rate monitor, cell phone, MP3 player, and whatever other modern gizmo you normally carry with you. You'll be amazed at how liberating it can be."

Mark has a very good point. Why be burdened with all that *stuff*? Consider Mark's suggestion and chuck the stuff one run a week to see how it feels. If you like it, you can add a second day. Or you can get rid of one accoutrement at a time until you are free. It would be simpler to go "cold turkey," of course, but not everyone is capable of making such a clean break. After all, like barnacles growing on the side of a shipwreck, you added the stuff one at a time, and the stuff might need to be scraped off one at a time until you can feel comfortable running easy and free.

To consider what kind of an effect this would have, take a moment to do a little research. Open Tom Derderian's *Boston Marathon* and page through the chapters dealing with the 1970s. Take a good look at some of the photos, and then take a look at some of the times that were being run in those days, including by Tom himself. The only accessories most runners used were watches, and they were watches with hands that went around the dial; digital watches hadn't yet been invented. Running was pretty simple and pure—and runners were generally faster than they are today.

Consider also that if you enjoy racing, the United States of America Track and Field (and subsequently the Road Runner Club of America) bans the use of electronic devices: MP3 players, cell phones, and such. So it's easier and more practical to wean yourself off the devices in your training before getting disqualified from a race because of your use of electronic devices.

Why hamper yourself with stuff that literally has nothing to do with running? You'll have plenty of opportunities when you're old and rushed to an emergency ward to have all types of monitoring devices hooked up to you. And then it will mean more, because it will impress the nurses ("My, oh my. A resting heart rate of 52. We don't see that in here very often. That's one healthy heart!").

Then, as the wise old coot you've become, you can look back in fondness and joy to perfect runs you experienced—runs that stand out for their sweetness and light—and lightness.

Nobody except Marshall Ulrich* needs to remember runs as a beast of burden or as a mobile emergency ward.

Simplify! Simplify!

Your running life brings the most to your life when it intrudes the least. You want your running life to affect the rest of your life in a positive way. The world gets more complicated every day, rushing forward at such a speed and in such complex ways that it is a challenge to keep up.

Some psychologists worry that life is speeding up so much that people simply cannot keep pace and are subsequently overstressed. The human brain is adaptable, but it can only adapt at a certain speed. It needs time and space to cope with change. Consider a swimmer who dives into the river and begins swimming upstream at the same speed the water is coming toward him. He is able to stay even with a spot on shore. But should the river swell and the flow pick up speed, the swimmer will likely be swept away by the current. It will simply overwhelm him.

In a similar way, the onslaught of more and more electronic devices is marvelous and overwhelming at the same time. The technology is impressive. Look at an iPhone and compare it to a 1983 Apple IIe computer. (You might be able to find a picture of an Apple IIe on the Smithsonian Web site.) At a cost of more than $3,000, the Apple IIe was a marvel of its day, but compared to a $250 iPhone, it is a relic.

Yet for all of its marvelousness, the iPhone creates something of a burden in the way it mesmerizes and intoxicates with its myriad of applications. (When I went to get mine, the salesgal went on for 45 minutes about everything it does; I had to interrupt her to ask if it also works as a phone, because she had never mentioned that function.) Watching some people with portable electronic devices is similar to watching drug addicts. They literally can't tear themselves away from them and actually begin getting depressed if they go five minutes without a chime sounding to tell them they have a text message or a call. That much tension from, and adoration of, a device isn't good for the human nervous system.

---

*From July 1 through July 4, 1999, Colorado's Marshall Ulrich, frequent winner of the Badwater 135 race across Death Valley and up the shoulder of Mt. Whitney, attempted to run, self-supported, from Badwater in the bottom of Death Valley to the peak of Mt. Whitney, 14,494 feet (4,418 m), a distance of some 150 miles (241 km). The wheeled contraption he constructed to cart his equipment weighed 225 pounds (102 kg). "For the first time in my life," Ulrich observed afterward, "harnessed to a cart weighing more than 200 pounds, I felt the bondage of the servant animals, and the important role they have played in increasing the quality of human lives. The bondage to that cart taught me how we are all united in the universe in spirit, none better than the other, none worse."

For all the talking and texting, smartphones are also alienating. One 15-year-old boy I know texts a girl in his school but has never spoken to her in person! People are communal animals. Face-to-face interaction is almost as important to good mental health as is eating. Interaction adds texture to life.

Running with others offers a sense of community and provides a release and a resource. It seems that no subject is too alien or too out of bounds when a small group of runners hits its stride on a long workout.

On the other hand, running alone frees a person's body and mind. For that period of time, the nervous system is relieved of its anticipation of electronic stimulation. This gives it a vacation, a nap, a rest from being bombarded by an increasingly infringing world. It also frees the mind to solve what may seem like insurmountable problems.

There is an almost magical aspect of running alone when not burdened with stuff. All of the day's complexities fall away, and problems that seemed overwhelming are stripped of their frills and brought down to the simplest of terms, from where they can easily be solved.

Many a noontime runner has come back to work astonished at the simplicity of a solution to a seemingly complex problem that had vexed her for hours at the office. The pure run leaves behind the white noise and the fuzziness of the problem and strips it bare. Bare is always easier. The burden is cut loose, and the runner runs free.

Can life get any better than that?

For Your Consideration

- Running is one of the simplest and most fundamental of activities. Keep it simple.
- The lighter a car can be made, the more efficient it is. Add weighty accessories and it burns more fuel, which undermines its performance.
- Allow your run to serve as a cleansing and liberating activity, not a burdensome chore.
- The rhythm of a long run allows you to clear the cobwebs and confusion from your head. Many a thorny question that seemed to have no answer is readily resolved during a run . . . if you give yourself the opportunity to ruminate.
- Learn to listen to the rhythm of your own heartbeat and breathing. It is as close to primal purity as we get in today's world, and one of the things that makes running so precious.

Eric Gevaert/fotolia.com

TAP THE ATHLETE

with

Kathrine Switzer

There is an oft-told parable about the restrictions we place on our-selves—with the help of those around us—that bind us to the earth for the rest of our lives and deny us physical heaven. The parable goes like this:

> There was a tall wall in town, the width of which was less than a dozen inches. The wall was higher than a man's head. It started at one end of a city block and went, unbroken, to the other end of the block. Kids used to climb on it by placing crates and boxes against the wall. One kid dragged his bike up the side of the wall and began to ride it along the top of the wall. His friends thought it was really cool. The kid very much enjoyed riding across the top of the wall. But one day, an adult who also happened to be a science professor of great renown came along and explained to the boy that he couldn't really do that—nobody could do that. It was impossible. The next time the kid tried to ride his bike along the top of the wall, he fell off and broke his arm.

Natural-born athletes are different from regular folks. They are born with an animal prowess that thrives deep in the muscles and sinew, below consciousness. They do what they do so well as a function of who they are—without thinking about it and analyzing it. If they think about it at all, it is more often to wonder why, in the area of their extreme compe-tence, the people around them are not as capable, and sometimes even downright inept. To them it doesn't seem natural that others fall short of the level to which they were born, even when they try their best.

We've all known these natural athletes and we've all envied them—the high school kid who instinctively knows where the opposing quarter-back is going to throw the football before it leaves his hands so he can get where he needs to be to steal it out of the outstretched hands of the intended receiver; the basketball player who can toss a three-pointer instinctively without thinking about it, who lofts the ball up and turns to run back downcourt without watching it go in because she already knows it is going to do just that (remember John Jerome, from the introduction of this book, throwing rocks at bottles?); the runner who explodes from the blocks and is three steps down the track before you or I have so much as reacted to the starter's gun. The list goes on and on and on and could be discouraging—if we let it.

The good news is that sport is an area in which hard work can some-times make up for talent, or in which real talent is awakened later in life. Good genes will take us only so far; sometimes hard work can take us farther.

Michael Jordan got cut from his high school basketball team. Wade Boggs went out to the ballpark early every day to work on his fielding.

To make up for a lack of natural talent, Emil Zatopek ran harder workouts than any human being could be expected to endure and as a result became one of only a handful of long-distance runners who could truly be called legendary.

There is an athlete in each of us. Most of us just haven't been introduced. Some people seem as afraid to meet the athlete in themselves as they are to explore dark corners of their psyches.

Being an athlete is a combination of mental attitude, some number of agreeable genes, and hard work. The sport and lifestyle of running are their own special case, though. For all of its incredible simplicity, there is no more profound or complex sport on the face of the earth. Consider its permutations and consider that there must be at least one permutation available to every mobile body on earth.

What other sport offers such latitude? At a track meet there are distances from 100 meters to 10,000 meters. On roads, there is everything from the urban mile to the urban marathon to (in New York City on a 1-mile loop) an annual 3,100-mile (4,989 km) race. Out in the country, there is everything from the 50-yard dash to the 100-mile trail race. There are 24-hour, 48-hour, 72-hour, and 6-day races at local tracks. There are adventure runs from Badwater in Death Valley to the peak of Mt. Whitney, 100-mile stage races along the base of the Himalayan Mountains, and transcontinental races from Los Angeles to New York. This is not even getting into cross-country races and running legs in triathlons and multisport events.

Genes will take you only so far on those running excursions. A strong will and firm resolve then take over, which are qualities any human being can develop by accessing the athlete within. Unfortunately, even some folks who search out the runner within and take up the act of running fail to search deep enough for the athlete within.

What does that mean? Simply, there are tens of thousands of runners in the United States who do as little as possible to get by. As a result, they never discover that there is a lot more to be tapped. Let me give you a very concrete example. I don't like to stress the marathon, but because very real statistics are available, it is easy to cite accurately:

- In 1979 there were 75,000 marathoners in the United States; in 2004 there were more than 400,000.
- In the 1979 Boston Marathon, 24 Americans ran under 2:18; in the 2004 Boston Marathon, no Americans (zero, zilch) ran under 2:18.

How is that possible? How can it be that from a pool of 75,000, 24 ran sub-2:18s at the world's most famed marathon way back in 1979 and more recently not one ran a sub-2:18 from a pool of over 400,000? It simply does not compute.

One could expect that, based on past performances (and ignoring the fact that we have enjoyed nearly 30 years of improved diet, running shoes, training methods, and so on), with over 400,000 marathoners in the country, there should have been 144 Americans under 2:18 at the 2004 Boston Marathon. What that says to me is that there are literally hundreds of national- and world-class American marathoners slogging around the streets who don't realize that they are national class and world class simply because they have never been encouraged or have never been self-motivated to reach in and yank out the athlete within by training harder and longer.

In an increasingly sedentary world, even runners seem frightened to tap into the trapped athlete within. Instead, they approach running tentatively, encouraged by many to take the path of least resistance combined with the American imperative of instant gratification: become an overnight marathoner with the bragging rights that go with it; then drop out the other side and move on to something else.

We see this constantly in one of the largest segments of would-be marathoners: charity runners. Charities require a constant supply of new runners to commit to secure pledges and then get trained to run a marathon. What happens to the runners on that journey or afterward is immaterial.

Virgin runners who have never run a step are trained to run a marathon within six months. Often, when they line up at the starting line, they've never run another race on the way to attempting 26.2 miles and they are still 30 to 40 pounds overweight. The results are preordained: they run a marathon, they acknowledge that it was the most incredibly difficult physical thing they've ever done or are likely to do, and they never run again. The athlete within never sees the light of day, and the romance of the marathon distance is undermined because it wasn't raced; it was survived. (This is not to say that all charity program coaches are inept. But if all of them were adept, there wouldn't be dozens—sometimes hundreds—of charity runners out on a marathon race course long after the course closes.) These runners are cheated out of becoming *runners*.

Dick Beardsley, who remains the fifth-fastest American marathoner of all time (he ran 2:08:53 against Alberto Salazar in the famous Duel in the Sun at Boston in 1982), took nearly five years to come back from injuries before he again lined up to run a marathon—and he's obviously got the genes of a champion. Yet he was smart enough to know that the body needs to build to longer distances, along the way sculpting the athlete within so when it is time to line up at the starting line, the athlete informs the runner.

In an age of obesity and sedentary lifestyles, the natural athlete in most of us is either buried under layers of fat or forever stilled by inertia. What

a crime it is, then, that so many potential world-class runners' careers are short-circuited by being pushed too far and too fast.

Nothing good is built overnight. The athlete, muffled by an increasingly antiphysical society, needs time to emerge and to shine. In the 1970s athletes were given time to mature, to come into their own. No one told them they couldn't do it. Their bodies were prepared by regular running, and their competitive spirit was nursed in short races and elevated as speed and distance gradually increased. The full term of matriculation was employed; there was no diploma mill in which they put a check in one end and received a hollow PhD at the other end.

You owe it to yourself to enjoy the full measure of your efforts, to meet and greet the athlete within, to run under that athlete's power and determination, and in the process to be genuinely fulfilled. All of this begins with the simplest of acts: Open the door and go for a run. Or start by going for a walk. Every time I walk out the door to go on a workout, I recall a saying my father used to overuse. When he wanted us to get out of the house, he'd tell us, "Go out and get the stink blown off you!"

The very act of going out the door and moving under your own power taps into the essentials of human evolution. The largest bones and muscles in the human body are in the legs for a very good reason: we were designed to move. In talking to groups of novice runners, I add to that the observation that if we were designed to sit in front of a television for hours, from an evolutionary standpoint, such an activity (or lack of same) would develop in us beautifully sculpted butts, but as we can observe, that isn't what happens.

What is the other design factor in the human being that makes us excellent walkers and runners? That would be our sophisticated cooling apparatus: our potential to use our skin as a cooling mechanism by sweating. No other animal on earth sports such a complex and efficient cooling system, which contributes to us being natural-born endurance athletes.

Consider that for a moment: Every human being on earth is designed as an endurance athlete. How good we are at being endurance athletes depends, as stated before, to some extent on genes. But a good deal of it also depends on hard work.

Anyone who is willing to put in the hard work can be a decent runner—perhaps not a world-class runner, but at least a decent runner. What other human activity can make that claim? Some of us could practice the piano until our fingertips bled and we'd never become a decent pianist. The same is true about doing math or repairing cars . . . or anything else. Some people are good at it, whereas others could devote their lives to trying to learn it and they'd never progress past pitiful. (All you need to do to see this proved beyond argument is to watch the early shows of *American Idol* each year.)

Running isn't like most other activities. Do it, then do it some more, and you can become decent at it. Do it a lot more, and you can probably become above average.

But, you may ask, what kind of an athlete could I possibly have trapped inside of me?

Consider the fact that there are blind runners (some of whom can run a marathon in under 3 hours), runners who are amputees (one gal not long ago ran a marathon in 3:05 as a below-the-knee amputee), runners with diabetes (who greatly benefit in controlling their disease through exercise), 85-year-old runners, and people who used to be runners who take it up again later in life who are changed forever by the rediscovery of how simple yet profound the act of running is.

Later in this book are discussions of how to greatly enhance your running by getting out of a rut and making sweeping changes to your running. This is not what we're addressing here. This is way simpler than that. This is about walking out the door and meeting your athlete. Go out there and spend some quality time with your new best friend, the athlete that was trapped inside you, the primitive eons-old runner who wants out, the essential runner ready and eager to reveal aspects of yourself that have long been repressed.

Millions of runners ply the world's highways and byways. They weren't always runners, except in the relatively rare instance in which they ran track and field or cross-country during their school days and continued to do so after graduation. Go to any local 5K race and hang around after the race is over and talk to a group of the runners. Ask them how they got into running. If there are eight people there, seven of them will reveal that they weren't athletes in high school. In each case they will be happy to confirm two things:

1. I never imagined that I was a runner until I became one.
2. I'm more comfortable with myself now that I'm a runner than I've ever been in my life.

The nice thing about running is that the runner is always there, patiently waiting to be released. There isn't a predetermined starting date or a firm expiration date.

One of the easiest ways to release the athletic beast inside and to keep it loose is to set running goals, both short term and long term. It's fine on occasion to just run around for the sake of basic movement, but to loosen the athlete, goals are necessary, both as a motivational factor (to get you out the door on days you'd rather not go) and as a testing factor (testing just how good you can be with a requisite amount of training).

Setting goals is a process that runs parallel with the personalities of most people who get involved in running, and it is a way of laying out

yardsticks end-to-end toward reaching a long-term goal. You may start with modest goals and grow from there. You may be surprised at how motivating reaching goals can be. Set a short-term goal and achieve it, and you will be doubly motivated to strive for the intermediate goal, and from there to the long-term goal.

One of the most impressive runners I've ever met, and a guy who really knows goals, is John Keston, who holds numerous age-group world records. He didn't begin running until he was 55 and, like many other people, he started running to whip himself into better shape (in his case, to play squash). He was a Shakespearean actor and professional singer, with a runner lurking inside him, just as one lurks inside all of us.

John began entering 10K races as a lark and found that, for his age, he was pretty good. Through dedication and hard work he became ever better and began setting records for his age. An aspect to consider with running, at least if you wish to race, is competition—against other runners and against yourself. Age-group competition occurs within the larger race; beyond that is competition against yourself, which involves setting PRs (personal records), trying to run faster and better than you did last week.

But getting back to John Keston and his fully emerged runner: John is doubly impressive because on a somewhat regular basis (like, once every five years or so), he has been forced to reinvent his runner as a result of a nonrunning accident (such as riding a bike over railroad tracks and breaking his hip to the point that it required a metal plate) that puts him on the disabled list for months at a time. Each time he has eased back into running and reemerged as good as ever and sometimes even better. He has essentially been reborn on a regular basis.

Even those with decades of experience can be reborn. Kathrine Switzer, one of the pioneers of women's running, twice the head of the Avon running program and the author of *Marathon Woman*, related this surprising and refreshing development in her own search for the inner athlete:

> When people would say to me, "I used to run, I don't anymore. I should get back to it. I always liked it," I used to be amazed. How on earth could you like running and not do it?
>
> Now, after running for 50 years, I think I understand a little better. The athlete within is always there; just finding it is often challenging.
>
> I never stopped running, and still define myself first as an athlete, but over the last 10 years I was spending less and less time actually doing it. Work, travel, fatigue, higher priorities—you know the story—all resulted in my running less. Consequently, I got slower, put on weight for the first time in my life, and was less confident of my physical capability. Well, hell, I was 60, *I told myself*. Of course I had less capability!

After running 35 marathons, it became more fascinating to do the TV commentary of the race. After thousands of miles of Sunday-morning long runs, using that time to write another book was more challenging to me. There was still joy and great creativity in my daily run, but it wasn't compelling enough to make me push myself.

And then a funny thing happened. Fascinating events began popping up that didn't exist even a decade ago. Like running on a game reserve in Kenya, or running three races in three days in Bermuda, or running over a mountain range over rough tracks and through rivers in New Zealand. I found myself wishing I could do them, and annoyed at not being 28 anymore. Back then, I only had to pull on my shoes and I was there. And now what? Was the old athlete somewhere inside me even capable of trying?

And then another funny thing happened. I was meeting women who were 65 and 70 years old who had just started running and were doing these events. Older than me! Way older than me! That was it; if they could do it, I could, too. For years I had the reputation for motivating others, and now, presto! They were motivating me. It's the truth: Finding the athlete inside happens quickly when you are inspired or when your competitive hackles are raised. The athlete was there inside raring to go; it just needed a goal to give me the focus.

The ongoing process has been funny, wistful, time-consuming, and extremely enlightening. Although the outcome has yet to be determined, I can say for certain that it is humbling to have to work so hard again; it is bewildering to still feel inside how I felt at 28 but how incapable I am of being anything but 63, how hilarious (you have to laugh) it is to have to spend twice as much time training now as I did then because it takes me twice as long to cover the same distance and because I need a nap afterward. But it is thrilling in the extreme to find that old lioness getting stronger again; perhaps a bit wobbly and flea-bitten but still roaring.

The athlete lurks in all of us. It is our human nature honed over tens of thousands of years. It is up to us to open the cage and let it loose. Even if it goes on hiatus, remember that it can still be revived and again released into the wild.

For Your Consideration

- Don't demand too much too soon, or you will court injury and burnout.
- Just because there is a distance known as the marathon doesn't mean you have to run it this year—or ever.

- Try different sports, and in running, try different distances. We all have sports or distances at which we are better than we are at others.

- Long-distance running is a sport and lifestyle that is ideal for those who are adept at delayed gratification. Delayed gratification—like the taste of the tree-ripened fruit—has more profound rewards than does instant gratification.

- It is never too late to seek the athlete within, nor too early to give that athlete his or her head.

Wojciech Gajda/fotolia.com

KEEP IT IN PROPORTION

with

Amby Burfoot

Recovering alcoholics and drug addicts make good long-distance runners. At least for a while. That's because they have the capacity—nay, the compulsion—to become obsessed with their habit of the moment, frequently to their ultimate detriment.

Good long-distance running requires a strong dose of dedication administered on a regular basis at increasingly larger amounts if it is to work. As with taking drugs, the more you increase your capacity, the more it takes to get a reaction—or, in the case of long-distance running, the more it takes to make even incremental improvements.

Numerous recovering alcoholics and drug abusers slide over to long-distance running as a substitute for their negative addictions. Besides helping them obsess about something other than drugs, long-distance running also contributes to keeping them away from smoking cigarettes, a seeming staple at most Alcoholics Anonymous meetings.

Long-distance running has long been touted as a positive addiction. It was initially referred to as such by William Glasser in the 1960s and made popular in his 1976 book of the same title.

Glasser cited running and meditating as positive addictions. He promoted both for their own sake and also as alternatives to negative addictions.

Even people who have not dealt with negative addictions who come to running tend to become, to varying extents, addicted to the activity. Why else continue to participate in an activity that from the outside appears to be insanely repetitive and profoundly boring? "I just like to do it. I have to do it. It makes me feel good and when I don't do it, I feel bad" sounds a bit lame, explains little (at least to those who don't run), and certainly makes you sound like an addict of some kind, but that response is very common among runners.

Some psychologists cite examples of running clients who exhibit classical physical signs of withdrawal when, because of injury, their running is temporarily taken away from them. Other psychologists point to the brain's release of endorphins during running, which are like a natural drug that allows a runner to turn a seemingly dull, boring, and repetitive activity into a holy rite. (Endorphins are morphine-like chemicals released by the brain under various circumstances, including long-distance running and sex. Some anthropologists have theorized that the release of endorphins was crucial to ancient people's survival because their release mediated the drudgery and discomfort of long-distance and long-running hunts for animals to be used as food.)

The only problem with addictions is that they are overpowering, and as such, they tend to ultimately get out of hand. They can take over control of the person rather than the person controlling (and using) them in a positive way.

In 1989 I wrote a book called *The Exercise Fix* (Human Kinetics). It was a study of the runner's high and of exercise addiction in general but in running specifically, because running offered the largest and most willing cohort available at the time. My conclusion was that regular aerobic exercise such as running is good for a person on many levels. It offers a plethora of positives: It increases physical endurance, provides more ready energy, controls weight, lowers blood pressure, releases stress, alters moods in a positive way, increases self-esteem and body image, increases the efficiency of the brain by infusing the brain cells with additional oxygen and nutrients, and builds up your T-shirt collection. But the book went beyond the positives to address what happens when running takes control of a person's life.

The Exercise Fix was inspired to some extent by the vitriolic response to an editorial Bob Anderson wrote in *On the Run*, a tabloid fortnightly publication of *Runner's World*, in which he said that to some people, running had become a religion. He got blasted by religious zealots as well as by those who were defensive about the amount of time they spent running. Bob's observations made perfect sense to me, but then, I was exposed to an awful lot of running crazies. This was, after all, 1978, when the first running boom was building toward a force-5 hurricane.

The fact that some of the respondents were so virulent about how their excessive running was not bad for them was fascinating. Of course, within the next five years, most of them were no longer runners. I wove this fact into the conclusion of *The Exercise Fix*: Those who run too much either burn out psychologically or run themselves into the ground physically by overdoing it and failing to listen to the cries of distress their chronically injured bodies bleat out.

As an aside, more fascinating still was the vehemence with which these former addicted advocates of running became the lifestyle's harshest critics. Their conclusion: *Running is bad for you, so don't do it. Look what it did to me.* They didn't say, *I ran to excess, didn't listen to my body, didn't listen to my doctor, didn't listen to my friends, and was a total jerk. Now look at me. I'm a near-cripple and I should be ashamed of myself. Don't do what I did. Ease into running, build gradually, listen to your body, and enjoy the process.*

Let's face it: There is only one future for a runaholic: to become an ex-runner.

If that's the fate you desire, run wild, run crazy, and run to excess. In fact, run to wretched excess. Your running career will be finite.

If you want running to be a part of your life for the rest of your life, keep it in perspective, and keep it in proportion to everything else in your life. Can running be an important aspect of your life? Certainly. Does it fulfill deep-seated needs for which the body was designed? It

does. Is it the be-all and end-all of your life? It shouldn't be. Not if you are running at a level that is healthy and allows for other aspects of your life to occasionally have sway.

Many converts to long-distance running allow it to take over their lives, to the extent that they lose their families and friends in the process because running becomes more important to them than anyone or anything else. That's unfortunate. When running has that large a role in your life, it has gotten out of hand. It is ruling your life, and you have lost control; when that happens, it's time to cut back or take some time off. If you don't, your body will revolt by courting injuries that bring your running life to a painful and bitter end.

How can you tell if your running has taken control of your life, rather than the other way around? Ask yourself the following questions:

- Do I feel guilty if I miss a day of running?
- Does my mood deteriorate if I don't get in my daily run?
- Am I likely to run through injuries?

There is a whole litany of questions you can ask yourself, and even after asking yourself these questions, you can still rationalize why you need to keep overdoing it. The following checklist can help you determine if you might have a running addiction.

Commitment or Compulsion?

In order to develop and maintain aerobic (cardiorespiratory) fitness, a person must practice the aerobic activity on a regular basis. Kenneth Cooper, father of aerobics, considers doing a 20-minute workout three or four times a week, or every other day, to be practicing aerobic fitness on a regular basis.

Aerobic practitioners who go beyond Cooper's minimum recommendations tend to participate in the activity for reasons other than good cardiovascular health. They find fulfillment in the fitness activity itself and not merely in the end result, which becomes a sort of by-product.

These more ambitious people tend to invest a good deal of time and commitment in training and racing, whether the aerobic activity is long-distance running or swimming, sustained bicycling, cross-country skiing, aerobic dance, or triathlon. Generally, these are laudable pursuits that provide an extreme degree of fitness to the athlete and provide an arena for socially acceptable personal fulfillment.

(continued)

A number of these people, however, consistently escalate their fitness pursuits until those pursuits become the center of their lives, displacing family, friends, sex, hobbies, and job in importance. The admonition that "too much of anything is not good for you" comes forcibly into play.

The following self-test is designed to gauge your attitude toward your involvement in aerobic pursuits. Some of the questions may not be applicable to you at this time in your aerobic career. For instance, you may never have consulted a sport therapist or sport psychologist, and to you the statement "My sport therapist is my best friend" may seem rather absurd. Consequently, you will likely place a score of 1 next to it.

Some of the statements refer to a specific type of aerobic pursuit (the triathlon) but are applicable to a variety of aerobic efforts, and presumably you will answer accordingly. Other statements are general: "If you don't even try, you've already lost." These have an obvious application to aerobic activities, and especially to aerobic competition.

A SELF-TEST

Where Exercise Addiction Stands in Your Life

On a scale of 1 to 10, with 10 being the strongest, give an objective weight to each of the following statements as they apply to you and your endurance fitness. Then total your numbers and see the interpretations at the end of the test. Fill the test out with a pencil, or make photocopies so you can retake it periodically.

_____ Aerobic fitness is important to me. I'm positive I'll be engaged in one or more endurance sports for the rest of my life.

_____ A day without an endurance workout is like a day without sunshine.

_____ If it becomes downright impossible to get my workout in today, I can always double up tomorrow.

_____ Until I get my workout in, I'm a real bear—as in unbearable.

_____ A little pain proves there's progress being made.

_____ If 5 hours of workout a week is good, 10 hours is twice as good.

_____ Warm-up and cool-down are important, but it's what comes in the middle of a workout that counts.

_____ As far as endurance training goes, more is always better.

_____ "My workouts for the past week? Glad you asked!"

_____ Regularity at any cost is the backbone of all fitness.

_____ Quality without quantity is wasteful.

_____ "My sport therapist is my best friend."

_____ You're not a real runner until you've done a marathon.

_____ Triathlons are important because they allow you to do more training with impunity.

_____ To go for more, always for more, is what's important in life.

_____ Rest is for the weary, not for the strong.

_____ An unbroken string of workouts should remain so.

_____ A person who has nothing to prove has already made a point.

_____ If you don't even try, you've already lost.

_____ Relaxation is all right _after_ you've made the grade.

_____ TOTAL YOUR SCORE.

Where does your total fall? 161-200, exercise addiction personified; 121-160, leanings toward exercise addiction; 81-120, nearly neutral; 41-80, fitness with a mellow bent; 10-40, approaching terminal mellow. Retake this test every four to six months.

Analyzing Your Score

What was your total for the test?

Let's briefly examine the various levels of involvement in aerobic activities indicated by the test results:

20-40. Very few people involved in aerobic activities are likely to score this low simply because, to pursue an aerobic activity, a certain commitment to regularity is necessary. Consequently, answering the first question truthfully is likely to put the typical aerobic exerciser well on the way to the next level.

41-80. A person who pursues aerobic fitness according to Cooper's minimum weekly requirements and who maintains fitness strictly for its health benefits is likely to fall into this category.

81-120. This range is referred to as neutral because it includes people who occasionally increase their training to take part in an annual competition or who typically increase their involvement in aerobic activities when the weather improves. People in this category tend to stay involved in aerobic fitness all year round, but to escalate the involvement on occasion as the spirit or season moves them.

(continued)

Commitment or Compulsion   *(continued)*

121-160. Most aerobic athletes fall into this category. They are involved in fitness for more than just the health benefits, and they regularly pursue competitive goals, whether that means trying to break 40 minutes in the 10K road race or doing three or four short-course triathlons per summer. This group also includes aerobic dancers who periodically gear up to reach higher levels and bicyclists who regularly train for and take part in century rides and other endurance events. Also included are cross-country skiers who compete in several citizens' races a year.

161-200. At this level, one's commitment to aerobic activities and sports tends to cross over into obsessive and compulsive behavior. Aerobic training becomes more important than nearly anything else in life. It is the focal point of each day. There is a tendency to willingly train through injuries and to compete in races when injured. There is also a tendency to blindly defend one's intense involvement on the basis of the benefits aerobic fitness bestows on the human body. The phrase "No pain, no gain" is used at first to get through difficult workouts, and later to justify training while injured.

It is advisable to retake the self-test periodically because, as with other addictions, aerobic involvement may go through peaks and valleys, binges and layoffs (often occasioned by temporarily debilitation injuries associated with the fitness activity).

The typical tendency, however, is for the person addicted to aerobic exercise to pursue that exercise in a headstrong and headlong fashion.

Running, at its best, should complement your life. It should keep you fit, relieve stress, provide healthy competition, help stave off diseases, give you more stamina to follow other pursuits in life, raise your self-esteem, keep you out of the doctor's office, and, let's face it, make you more virile and increase your life expectancy. Running can be a simple activity that benefits every corner of your life while undermining nothing. It can easily be integrated into your daily life, no matter how busy you are.

Running, which can feel at the outset like an intrusion into your life that you must shoe-horn into a daily routine, can eventually come to be as natural and as second nature as combing your hair—if you happen to have hair to comb. Running can be one of those daily habits that fall by the wayside unless you integrate it into your daily life.

Daily running and walking used to be an integral part of the average life of just about every man, woman, and child on earth. In the ancient world, travel by foot was a given because horses and elephants hadn't yet been domesticated. Many tribes were nomadic and people traveled great distances on their own two feet. In those days, walking and running weren't integrated into daily life; daily life was integrated around the physical activity of getting from one place to the next.

Even when various animals were domesticated, not everyone had a horse to ride. Twenty-five hundred years ago, the majority of the Athenian army traveled on foot. The hoplites (light infantry) were trained to run a fast mile while wearing their armor. This training made them more maneuverable and therefore more effective, as they proved at the Battle of Marathon against the much more numerous Persians (today's Iranians) in 490 BC.

In Rome, the common folk did not speed around the city on chariots, knocking Nubian slaves out of the way; chariots were only for the very rich and powerful. The same goes for the fancy carriages in Europe and the Orient several hundred years ago. On our own Western frontier, the pioneers typically walked beside their oxen- and horse-drawn wagons and ranged far and wide on foot pursuing game along the trail. It is only within the last 50 or 60 years that nearly every family in the United States has owned a car—even the poor and downtrodden. Even today, though, most people in developing countries still get to where they are going by traveling on foot.

In the developed world, around the middle of the 20th century, running was considered a form of punishment. Going on forced marches toughened up soldiers; they were frequently treated to the "dog trot," alternating walking and jogging. On high school and college football teams, miscreants were forced to run laps as punishment. The same went for baby boomers in physical education classes in the 1950s and 1960s: Goof up or goof off and it was laps around the gym for you.

Only since the 1970s, and only among a certain elite, has running been seen as a reward and sometimes as an alternative to riding in or driving a car. Although the object of derision among many in the car culture of the 1970s, Frank Shorter made running cool for postcollegiates who wanted to maintain some level of fitness in a society where, for most college graduates, physical work was being phased out.

During the initial running revolution (then thought of as a fad that would fade), somehow a relatively high number of college graduates who had salaried jobs (jobs that also went well beyond the standard 40-hour workweek) were able to fit running into their busy professional and social lives. People who were not world- or national- or even regional-class competitors were running 50, 60, and 70 miles a week. Somehow

they managed to make their regular running an integral part of their lives without missing a beat.

These early runners fit running into their lives by making it a priority. Running every day was no longer an option; it was a necessity. A day without running became an incomplete day. They simply, over a period of time, raised the status of their daily run until it just had to be done. To some it went so far, as we discussed earlier in this chapter, as becoming an obsession.

If you have not yet made the commitment to running, such dedication may seem almost cultish, and therefore beyond your capacity. But consider how easily we get ourselves into other habits that we either consciously or unconsciously integrate into our daily lives. Do you stop at a cafe on the way to work to get a fancy cup of coffee? Do you go by a convenient store on the way to work to pick up a donut? Do you check e-mails first thing in the morning, and every hour thereafter? At lunch, do you go to the same deli or fast-food joint and order pretty much the same thing every day? Such habits are relatively easy to develop, and once formed, can be difficult to break.

This is not to say that there aren't sacrifices to be made on the way to integrating a regular running program into your week. You may have to get up an hour earlier to get in an early-morning run before work, or you might have to give up socializing with fellow workers over lunch so you can go out for your daily run. Fortunately, it is usually easy these days to find someone at work who'll want to go along with you on your noon run. It may surprise you how little time it takes to develop a new, healthier habit that works running into your daily life.

In the same way, you'll want to examine how you can best integrate your weekly long run into your weekend. So as not to disrupt the family's weekend schedule, many a runner gets up before the rest of the family and gets the run out of the way. By using the term "get it out of the way," I don't mean to suggest that a long run is odious or a chore. For some runners, that Saturday or Sunday early-morning run is the only hour or two they have alone. Free time in the current rushed world is often a godsend—an hour or two of sanity and a reward for a week well spent with other people doing other duties.

Running can also serve as a perfect stress reliever, whether done alone or with others. If asked to choose between an hour run or an hour on an analyst's couch, many will choose running, hands down. Even some analysts are prone to agree. In his essay "Jogotherapy: Jogging as Psychotherapy," in the book *Running as Therapy,* Frederick D. Harper wrote: "The theoretical approach of 'jogging as psychotherapy' is predicated on the supposition, supported by empirical evidence, that jogging can alter psychological states and psychological traits" (Sachs and Buffone, p. 83).

Make running a virtue that you use to complement your life, to promote your general health, and to get out and explore new worlds. And occasionally, take a break. Also, be sure to keep it all integrated but also in proportion. Your body (and your psyche) will thank you.

Amby Burfoot, winner of the 1968 Boston Marathon and editor-at-large at *Runner's World*, has been running competitively since high school back in the 1960s. Looking back at his long career as a runner, he put it into perspective this way:

Many years ago I thought Perfection was the only path, and in my running I sought to achieve it over all else.

I ran 20-milers on Sunday morning. On Sunday afternoon, I added up my mileage for the week. If it didn't total 100 or more, I ran the additional distance Sunday evening. I did hills on Tuesdays, and speed work on Thursdays. Saturday was a race day: I went out fast, and then picked up the pace. Every Monday morning, I started all over again.

For a while, my system appeared to be working. Distant stars came into focus. I set my sights ever higher. Olympic gold didn't seem out of reach.

Then I crashed. Over and over again. I learned life's lessons, and running's, the hard way. The stars receded, and my Olympic dreams grew tarnished.

But something good also happened. I figured out how to run on terms that actually worked. They didn't require Perfection. And sure, they didn't deliver impossible dreams.

But they made me happy. And I can live with that. I learned that:

1. No one ever completes an unblemished training plan. Some days you get sick. Other days you just feel like crap (even though you don't know why). The most you can hope for is that you'll hit 80 percent of the workouts you originally planned. And guess what? That's more than good enough. This led me to the 80 = 99 rule. If you do 80 percent of your planned workouts, you've got a 99 percent chance of hitting your goals. The other 1 percent depends on the weather, which you can't control at all. So let it go.

2. You can't be in top shape all the time. Sometimes you have to be in really crummy shape. (An excellent time for this is the Thanksgiving Day to Super Bowl period. And you don't lose any points if you extend to Valentine's Day. Or St. Patrick's Day. Or Easter. Personally, I don't think you should stretch things out past Easter. It just doesn't seem right. Besides, you might have to put on a bathing suit as early as June.)

3. Every year, month, week, and day marks a new beginning. And each is a really good time to, um, begin anew. No one's keeping score

but you, so you might as well play by whatever rules will help you suc-ceed. I'm not suggesting you set the bar low; I'm just suggesting you set the bar at a height you can clear. When he was close to death from prostate cancer, Dr. George Sheehan, the philosopher king of running, told me: "There's only one runner in your race, and you are he."

I've tried to take Sheehan's teaching to heart. I'm not striving for Per-fection any longer. I'm just trying to run the best I can in my own race.

Amby's conclusion is one he earned from decades of running and learning about both himself and the sport. As long as we do the best we can do, there's not much more we can—or should—expect of ourselves.

For Your Consideration

- Consider scheduling regular one- or two-week vacations from run-ning during which you don't run at all. These are the downtimes of your annual training cycle and will help you come back to the sport refreshed, in mind and body.

- Always be willing to ask yourself this question: Am I in charge of my running, or is my running ruling my life? If the latter is the case, you need to take a break and regroup.

- Ask yourself on occasion whether your personal life has expanded or shrunk since you took up running as a sport and a lifestyle.

- Observe yourself in social situations. Do you constantly bring up running as a topic of conversation? Is your next run too often on your mind? When is the last time you and your family and friends took a vacation that didn't involve running?

- Do you become anxious and ill natured if you don't manage to get in your run?

MAINTAIN A JOURNAL

with

Joe Henderson

What did you do four months ago in your training that helped you pull off that PR (personal record) at last weekend's 10K? What was your sequence of training? What were the key workouts? What days did you take off to properly recuperate? What additional racing did you do that might have contributed to your peaking at just the right time?

And how did you know exactly where you were on the night of June 4, 2005, when the prosecuting attorney had you under oath in the breaking and entering trial?

Well, that's easy. You've been keeping a running/life journal for the past decade, so you are able to access every workout you did for the 18 weeks leading up to that successful marathon, and you are able to provide an alibi for the night of June 4, 2005, because you were eating pizza and drinking beer at the Red Hawk Brewpub & Pizza Parlor after your usual weekly track workout with a dozen members of your running club.

Journals can be either valuable (think of Boswell's journal of the life of Samuel Johnson) or ridiculous (think of the shaggy-haired guy over there at the end table in the corner coffee shop who writes into his computer journal all day long, which means he writes about stroking the keyboard of his computer all day long). Many journals are fascinating. As interest in novels (other than genre novels) slowly expires, memoirs are all the rage—and they aren't all memoirs of famous people. Some are of seemingly normal people who have either inflated their lives beyond all recognition or lived secret lives nobody around them knew anything about.

A running journal is invaluable on two wildly different counts:

1. It can help you recreate a sequence of training that resulted in success so you can once again have a wonderful racing experience.

2. It can offer revealing clues as to how your training may have contributed to an unwanted outcome, such as an injury that took you out of the game for a goodly period of time right in the middle of the prime racing season.

The journal reveals all, the good and the bad. The nuts-and-bolts portion of your daily journal is merely a recitation of facts: how far you ran, how long you ran, at what speed you ran, what kind of weather you ran in, whether you warmed up first, whether you did an adequate cool-down, whether you did postrun stretching exercises, and so on. On the subjective side, you can note how you felt during the run and how well you recovered after the run.

Your journal allows you to examine your running life and learn from it so that you can improve your training and racing in the future, and increase the length of your running life.

Some runners want only facts in their daily journals: time, distance, pace, and so forth. For others a journal is a place to record the objective facts of their daily run, as well as a space to define their day by including the major events in their life that day as well as to comment on the day in general and on specific parts of it.

I began keeping a journal when I returned to running on June 13, 1977. I kept it in a three-ring binder. If I was in a hurry that day, I'd quickly write the basics of my running in the upper left corner; then make some observations on the day. If I had more time, I'd run the page through my Royal standard typewriter and go on at length about that day's run, that day's trials and tribulations at the office, and a few things personal.

The three-ring binder was perfect because I could add pages to it at will. When I had too many pages, I bought a second three-ring binder and began inserting pages there. Many of the long-term runners I know have a similar method of keeping their journals, but they use one three-ring binder per year. They are more meticulous that way than I am. My three-ring binder gained a companion binder only when the first binder wouldn't hold any more pages.

Eventually, though, I changed over to simple 3-by-5 cards, which I found I was using for a lot of things in my life, such as keeping a list of things I needed to do that day. The 3-by-5 cards were perfect because they were very portable (I could shove a handful of them into my back pocket when I was going on a trip) and very easy to file. At the end of the year, I used a felt-tip marker to scrawl the year onto the top card, and then I simply bound them with twine and put them into a box with bricks of cards from previous years.

The 3-by-5 cards held my daily workout in the upper left corner, and notes about the rest of the day filled out the rest of the card. If I needed to use the back of the card, that was OK, but I tried to use only the front of one card each day. That seemed like a good exercise in discipline and brevity.

My journals proved extremely valuable when a few years ago I attempted to recreate for *Marathon & Beyond* my most unforgettable ultramarathon: the 1978 Cow Mountain 50-Mile Planet Earth. It was fascinating going back through the journal. Because the race involved a whole weekend (getting there, camping out, getting up early to run it, partying afterward, and getting back home), there were three pages of notes, one for each day. Some of what I found in the journal did not jibe with what I remembered about the race weekend. You know how our memories, left to their own devices, edit events in our past to either mitigate them or to enlarge them. Well, the journal tells it like it was, because it was written in the heat of the moment in black and white.

When John J. Kelley, winner of the 1957 Boston Marathon, writes stories for our magazine about various marathons he ran, he can recreate them with great detail because he has kept a journal of his running and his life for decades. Clarence DeMar, seven-time winner of the Boston Marathon, kept meticulous records of his workouts and used them as a resource when he wrote his autobiography, *Marathon*.

Bruce Fordyce, from South Africa, still holds the 50-mile world record, which he set in Chicago in 1984. While writing a story on the 25th anniversary of Bruce's epic race, Rich Limacher exchanged e-mails with Oonagh, Bruce's sister, who had this to say about Bruce's journal keeping:

> Something that no one realizes about Bruce is that he is incredibly disciplined. He has kept a diary of his life, writing a page every day since he was 7 years old! That is part of his success. You should ask to see his running journals: they are incredible. Everything is noted, all the smallest details. Strangely, I once had the honour of sitting next to Sir Roger Bannister at a dinner party and got talking to him about how he broke the 4-minute mile. Poor man must be sick to death of that conversation, but he was so charming and told me he did it differently from others because he recorded all the details of his training, etc. So maybe they have that in common (*Marathon & Beyond*, May/June 2010, p. 126).

Maybe all of us would do well to have journal keeping in common with John J. Kelley, Clarence DeMar, Bruce Fordyce, and Sir Roger Bannister. Obviously, it worked well for them.

These days the process of keeping a journal has been made easy by the availability of commercial running journals. Joe Henderson publishes a nice one through Barnes & Noble.

Of course, as with many things these days, computer software exists for journal keepers. Also, smartphones can record and track your runs, which saves you the trouble of having to do the math to figure out your pace, because the software does it for you. Some applications can even create maps (with mile points) of your runs by tapping into GPS satellites.

Someday, you may want to write your memoirs (everyone seems to be doing that these days). It can often be somewhat disconcerting to think back to something that happened to you 10 years ago, jot down the details, and then go back and pull out your journal where the facts are lodged. The mind can do some strange gymnastics with facts if you give it 10 years to ruminate.

Keeping a journal has four benefits:

1. It provides the opportunity to keep a record of your daily life.
2. It offers an opportunity to chart your daily training to get the bigger picture.
3. It forces you to write every day, which can help you clarify what happened in your day.
4. Older journals are fun to read and often reveal insights into life that you have long since forgotten. And heck, if you have kids, it's a wonderful legacy to pass on to them. All sorts of organizations are running around attempting to extract meaningful memoirs from people who lived through World War II before they are gone. Your journal leaves a personal legacy that can be enjoyed while you are still alive and hopefully after you are gone.

It is worth taking the time to start a journal. If you decide to start a journal and it is the middle of the year, that's OK. You can start the journal today. Think of the upside: you can probably go to the local bookstores and buy a running journal for this year that's half price because half the year is gone.

Make a record of your running—and of yourself. Running buddy Joe Henderson has literally kept a running journal/log/diary for decades. Joe is the author of more than 20 books on running and served as the editor of *Runner's World* for seven years during its very formative period, 1970 to 1977. I asked him for some insights into the art and science of writing it all down:

You can be your own biographer. You don't need to be a talented writer to profit from a diary. You don't need to spend more than a minute a day writing in it. You don't even have to write many, or indeed any, words. Numbers alone tell stories as they help you recall old training sessions and suggest new possibilities. That process begins with three guidelines:

1. Keep it simple. Limit the amount of information to a few essentials that you can list briefly, quickly, and in an accessible form for review. The harder it is to keep a diary, the less likely you are to use it. You don't need a preprinted training diary. A calendar with large blocks of space for each day will do nicely as long as it is tacked to your bedroom or office wall, but it won't travel or store well. A notebook works best for this purpose. Fill it at the rate of one, two, or a few lines a day.

2. Keep it up. Analyze the accumulating data over extended periods to judge your results. Review at the end of each week, month, and year.

The longer you maintain the diary, the clearer your patterns of response to the exercise—and the clearer your thinking about it—become. Days of training leave behind what appear to be random footsteps in the diary. You can't take much direction from them at first. But the weeks, months, and years form a trail that points in two directions. It shows where you have been and where you might go next.

3. Keep it. Store your records in a safe place, treating them as the precious volumes they will become in time. Their value grows along with their age and bulk. The ultimate value of a diary is as a personal library of dreams and memories. You can open it to any old page and bring a day back to life. You can call up a mental videotape and, from a few statistics on the page, recreate all you did and felt that day. These recordings give substance and permanence to efforts that otherwise would be as temporary as the moment and to experiences that would be as invisible as footprints on the pavement.

For Your Consideration

- Don't put it off another day. Either buy a commercial running journal or put together one of your own, and start filling it in on a daily basis.

- Keep an accurate record of your daily runs, and be sure to record how you felt before, during, and after a run. Sometimes the best way to learn about the outcome of a long training period is to read about your perceptions of your running on specific days. If you ran a set workout but felt really beat up afterward, that's obviously an indication that you weren't getting enough rest.

- Think of your journal as a ship's log. Record the basics of what happened to you on that day. But unlike the dry jotting in a ship's log, your journal entries can come to life by adding your own observations and opinions.

- Find a safe, easily accessible place to maintain your journals. They don't take up all that much space, and you may need to consult them on a regular basis.

- Designate someone to whom the journals are to be given after you die. They will constitute one of your most valuable possessions and will be valued by someone in your family.

TAKE YOUR MEASURE BY RACING

with

Hal Higdon

You've probably seen them on your training runs: runners who, you can intuit by their pace or their clothing or their style, are running . . . just to run! You can't imagine that they've ever pinned on a number, toed a starting line, and raced against their peers on a timed and measured course. They constitute the Henry Thoreaus of the running world: running to their own iPod, marching to their own drummer, smelling the flowers, and damn the torpedoes that go whizzing by. They get by running on the periphery of running society, like ghosts or shadows.

It's difficult to determine whether these runners are serene or oblivious. We have several of them in our neighborhood. One young fellow, around 25 or so, runs in gray sweatpants, a blue sweatshirt, and a navy hat—the same outfit all year long, winter or summer. Another one, in his early 30s and sporting a dark beard, runs in baggy, dark blue shorts and a sweatshirt and wears clunky black high-top shoes that look as though they weigh 12 pounds each. I wave at them as they go by, but they seldom pay attention to me—they seem lost in their own little worlds.

Of course, I'm not much better. While I'm evaluating their sartorial conundrums, I'm as often wearing a pair of khaki pants as not. I don't go very fast anymore and don't see the need to be spiffy and high-tech. On days when I see both these guys, I think about stopping them so we three can form the Luddite Running & Pizza-Eating Society. The sassy running clothing industry ain't getting rich off us.

In years past I've felt a tinge of sadness for runners of this ilk. They seem content, like grazing cows, when they should be pushing themselves to be brazen like snorting bulls. They seem to be missing the cherry on the sundae: racing. But I've reined myself in these days, just as I no longer stop my car when I see a runner training on concrete sidewalks when there is a perfectly good asphalt bike path in the street, where the running surface is only about 25 percent as damaging.

My friends who race on a regular basis look at these shadow people and shake their heads in sadness, wondering what the point is of regularly putting in all those miles and then not putting them to good use in a contest of strength, sweat, and speed. My racing friends construct various analogies for these raceless runners:

- It's like writing two-thirds of a novel and then putting it in a drawer where nobody will ever see it.
- It's like buying a sports car and locking it in the garage.
- It's like working your way through college and then skipping final exams *and* missing out on graduation.

OK, OK. I'm being snide toward my racing friends. I have been, on many an occasion, one of them, and have taken away more from a race

than I've left of myself on the roads; that is, I've gained more satisfaction from running with a number rather than merely doing a workout of the same length.

What racers don't understand about "mere runners" is that, to runners, running is not a step to racing, not a training ground for a racing venue, but rather an end in itself. We all know it intellectually. Running lessens daily workplace and family stress, maintains a healthy body weight, confers a level of fitness, controls blood pressure—it bestows a bandoleer of health and fitness benefits.

After all, this is the modern world. We are no longer required to run from saber-toothed tigers or to chase down our next meal to survive. We have the privilege of running merely to run—for the simple, elemental joy of it. In the modern, more laid-back era, we have evolved away from Ernest Hemingway's definition of sport. To Hemingway, there were only three sports: mountain climbing, bull fighting, and auto racing; everything else was a game, he contended, because there was little chance of losing your life playing basketball or soccer . . . or chess. No more saber-toothed tigers, no more "sport" to running, according to Hemingway.

If someone is perfectly happy just running around the neighborhood three or four days a week, let 'em alone, right? If this were the 1970s, I'd be inclined to leave well enough alone. After all, the people who were running back then were generally competing nearly every weekend they could find a race, and they were getting pretty damned good at racing. Almost everyone who ran also raced—and raced quite well. They were wringing from their running the full measure of what it had to offer.

Racing can be an exhilarating experience. Training for a race can be a character-building process. And feeling good about yourself after you race can bestow confidence that extends to other aspects of your life.

Training for a race and then competing raises you physically above 95 percent of Americans. Even with the increasing number of people who enter road races in America, in the middle of the demographic curve and at the opposite end of it, there are enormous piles of people building blubber and perfecting inertia.

Besides improving their running fitness levels, racing exercises runners' psychological side. Preparing for and completing a race constitutes a significant event in a person's life, which is why some runners compete as often as they can, in spite of the fact that they will never outright win a race.

Mihaly Csikszentmihalyi's book *Flow: The Psychology of Optimal Experience* has a second subhead: *Steps Toward Enhancing the Quality of Life.* Csikszentmihalyi cites Roger Caillois, a French psychological anthropologist who divides games into four categories. The first category is *agon*: games that have competition as their main feature. "In *agonistic* games,

the participant must stretch her skills to meet the challenge provided by the skills of the opponents. The roots of the word 'compete' are the Latin *con petire*, which means 'to seek together.' What each person seeks is to actualize her potential, and this task is made easier when others force us to do our best" (pp. 72-73). With trying our best comes a right to grasp self-esteem.

George Sheehan, a cardiologist who for many years before his death in 1993 was considered the running guru, put it quite simply in his 1975 book *Doctor Sheehan On Running*: "Even for the free man, life is a dangerous and difficult game. Man, the player, must train long and hard before he can move through life with the simple, certain, leisurely grace of the expert. Still, it is the only game in town" (p. 185).

Old Doc Sheehan tested himself as often as he could by lining up at the starting line of any race he could find, from the mile to the marathon. He attempted to live the philosophy that Ortega y Gasset espoused: "Life is a dangerous struggle to succeed in being in fact that which we are in design" (p. 12). Doc Sheehan loved Ortega and quoted him often.

We are designed physically to move under our own power. We are designed psychologically and spiritually to compete with others and with our environment—and especially with ourselves. In the world not that long gone, we lived, therefore we competed; we competed, therefore we lived. These days we do it in the dating arena, we do it at work, we even do it against ourselves—hence the concept of the personal record.

Applied to the running universe, is it too simple to say that we sometimes use racing as a tool toward better racing? Let's take a moment to look at this concept. Two runners of equal talent and training will produce very similar results. Real-world testing like that tends to place us where we belong on the performance spectrum. But a sub-par race performance by a runner who is merely using the race as a hard workout does not diminish him relative to his twin who goes out to his best on that day. Their goals are entirely different.

Unless we are using a long race as a long workout toward a race further down the road, every race day is a test day. Although all such tests provide very objective results, not all tests constitute the be-all and end-all for all runners, although they could and perhaps should be.

Except for speed workouts at the track, most marathoners never test themselves in a 400-meter race, or an 800-meter race, and probably not a mile, either. At the other extreme are runners who specialize in shorter distances and have never and will never run a marathon, much less an ultra.

Besides the collateral benefit of increasing basic leg speed, distance runners who train for and compete at shorter distances can use those tests to predict their performances at upcoming longer-distance events.

Also, by testing themselves at shorter distances on an annual or even twice-a-year schedule, they can chart improvements in or the devolution of their racing skills.

It is commonly accepted that people who take up long-distance running and get serious about it can expect to improve for roughly 10 years. After the 10 years, aging and wear-and-tear tend to produce slower performances at all distances. So, for the novice runner or the returning runner, scheduling an annual time trial at shorter distances is often a mood elevator because the times continually improve.

Of course, after that decade of improvement, a runner can become dismayed and discouraged when charting the gradual and then escalating decline in performance. I know quite a few long-distance runners who threw in the towel when their times began to slip. This is unfortunate because everyone's performances slip as they age, which is why there is such an interest and participation in age-group running.

Because we are often our own harshest critics, we can find that competing against ourselves is the most difficult competition we face in life. For this reason, seriously consider scheduling shorter races to test yourself as a rite of passage every year. You can then work the tests into your broader buildup toward your next long race or marathon.

Because you want to do well in the test, don't sign up for a mile race if you haven't been doing shorter, faster workouts at the track. Plan to build toward your mile test or your 5K test with the same avidity you bring to your longer-distance training.

Many areas of the country have what are called all-comers track meets on a regular basis. These events are run like regular track meets, with the whole smear of events, but the races are open to anyone who wants to take part. There may be a nominal fee for taking part in a race, but it is usually quite inexpensive.

If you're going to do a mile race, for example, start building toward it three or four weeks in advance by religiously going to a track once or twice a week to do some step or pyramid workouts. (A pyramid workout involves running 400 meters hard, then jogging either a half lap or a full lap, then running 800 meters hard, jogging another lap, running 1,200 meters hard, jogging one lap, running 800 meters hard, jogging a lap, and finishing with a hard 400 meters.)

If you are shooting for a mile race, you don't necessarily have to do hard mile repeats. Working up to three laps hard should be enough, because based on your weekly mileage, you should already have an endurance base built up. If you've never done a mile race before, when you come out the other end of your fast four laps, you'll have a whole new appreciation for those runners who specialize in the event. Although it is only 1/26th of a marathon, it offers its own challenges, and unlike

a marathon, doesn't offer 25 additional miles in which you can make corrections for going out too hard in the first mile.

The mile can be a bear of a race, especially if you go out too fast in the first lap and the bear jumps on your back somewhere toward the end of lap 3 and you still have another lap to go—a lap in which you're supposed to pick up the pace to the finish line.

Any short track race is a perfect means of teaching your legs to turn over at a faster clip, which translates into more efficiency and speed at longer distances. This is especially true of 5K and 10K races. By increasing your leg turnover and improving your stride, you can make major improvements in both your races and your longer runs.

You can also use events shorter than the marathon to realistically predict what kind of time you can expect in your next marathon. It is somewhat easier to predict your marathon time from a recent 10K or half-marathon. For instance, if you are training for a marathon with a decent weekly mileage and a long run at least every other weekend, and all other factors remain equal, by running a 37-minute 10K, you should be able to break three hours in the marathon. A 40-minute 10K translates to a 3:30 marathon; a 45-minute 10K, to a four-hour marathon; and a 50-minute 10K, to a 4:30 marathon.

Using a half-marathon is even easier. Take your half-marathon time and multiply it by 2.1 for a realistic marathon finish time.

You can also test or measure yourself on what have become your well-established longer training courses. Most of the great road racers of all time had a favorite (or, in some cases, an infamous) longer training course that they would run as hard as they could in the weeks before their scheduled marathon to get a feel, in real numbers, of how well trained they were and how well they would do in the actual race. Some of them used familiar courses so they could check their journals to compare their present times against similar attempts in the past. Other top marathoners went to the track and ran 15 or 20 kilometers to get an accurate gauge of where they were in their fitness level.

Whether you go to a track or test yourself against last year's version of yourself at the same distance, or use the test as part of the formula for predicting your next race time, the by-products (faster leg turnover, more efficient stride, better biomechanics) are a bonus that will effectively make you a better—and much faster—runner than you were before you began taking the measure of yourself.

Let's take a moment to explain that by-product thing.

Although now retired, the British/French-designed Concorde airliner was a paragon of speed in its time. It roughly halved the time it took to fly from New York City to London or Paris. Once airborne, the plane looked as sleek as an arrow, but on the ground, it was awkward

looking, with its nose pointed to the tarmac. To increase the lift at takeoff, the nose tilted forward, which made it look like a heron that had been broken over the knee of a giant. Once the Concorde gained enough altitude, hydraulics pulled the nose into line with the rest of the plane's body, and it was ready to break the sound barrier—several times over.

It is similar with running long distances. When you jog at a slow speed, as we often do during warm-ups and cool-downs, there is a great deal of inefficient vertical movement, a lot of bouncing. You tend to use nearly as much energy bouncing as you do moving forward. Increase the speed gradually, however, and the body—like the Concorde—tends to smooth out: the stride lengthens, there is more forward movement, the up-and-down diminishes. You have slipped from jogging into running. You have become more biomechanically efficient. The increased forward movement comes from incorporating a longer stride; you cover more ground with each stride, so even if you keep the same leg turnover, you are faster and you cover more ground.

If you do speed work (at the track, by racing, by doing fartlek training) often enough, the better biomechanics and longer stride length will filter into even your more casual, slower runs. You will finish your long runs faster than you used to because you are covering more ground with each stride.

Speed work also makes it more comfortable to increase leg turnover, so that even your slow long runs are not as slow as they were. You have slowly ingrained a faster, more efficient form of running into your training.

If you've been running for quite a few years, you can notice this pleasant phenomenon by monitoring your foot strikes. When slowly jogging, you were likely landing on your heels, which in itself is inefficient because by doing that, you are essentially braking your forward movement with each stride. As you become more Concorde-like, you'll notice that you are striking farther along your foot, frequently midfoot, which is more efficient because you are releasing the brake that came with each stride. You are overriding it.

Take the measure of yourself by racing at shorter distances on a regular basis. After you've done it for a while, compare the sole wear on your training flats to that of the old pair in the back of the closet that you used when you were mostly jogging. The wear patterns should have changed noticeably.

For more discussion of the benefits of running distances that you may have considered unlikely or unusual in your running routine, visit http://tinyurl.com/35gl7mg for a bonus online chapter devoted to running unusual distances.

Hal Higdon is a contributing editor for *Runner's World* who's been racing for more than a half-century. One of his most recent books is a novel, titled simply *Marathon*. For training information from Higdon, go to www.halhigdon.com. (Hal is the guy who, in 1977, pushed the *Runner's World* owner/publisher to hire me to replace Joe Henderson as editor. I've since forgiven him.)

I asked him for his take on the value of racing. He wrote the following under the title "In Praise of Races":

> *Racing is to running as seasoning is to food. Pasta just does not taste as good without a layering of marinara. Tacos without salsa are, well, tacos without salsa. If you eat Mexican sans salsa, you won't have to quench the fires in your mouth with ice water, but you might as well be eating dog food.*
>
> *Thus, runners intent on finishing their first marathon may be missing some of the fun if they bypass shorter-distance races. More the problem, they may arrive at the marathon starting line unprepared for what is about to hit them.*
>
> *The racing experience does differ from the training experience. To race, you need to do more than just roll out the front door and start running. You often must travel, which in today's era of tightened security is not always a pleasant experience. You must know what to bring, everything from extra safety pins to gels to lubricants for your armpits. And don't forget your racing shoes.*
>
> *Racing means learning not to line up near the front row when you are a walker. It means learning how to cope with portable toilet lines. Racing means learning that you pin your number on the front, not the back. Didn't anybody tell you? And how do I affix this timing chip to my shoe?*
>
> *I submit that you learn by making your mistakes in small races, where the penalty for error is not severe. It's better than doing so in a 40,000-runner marathon for which you have trained eighteen or more weeks.*
>
> *Those of us who coach novice runners sometimes are troubled by the large numbers who appear at marathons with their bodies well trained but not yet their minds. They arrive at their first starting line not yet fully aware of the demands of the sport. That someone would run a first marathon also as a first race astounds us and also, to be honest, somewhat offends us. Yet we do not wish to insult new runners and guilt-trip them into following our rules (Our way or the highway). Yet the highway is 26.2 miles long, not all that easy to traverse if you skip some of the homework.*
>
> *Fortunately, in recent years more runners have begun to recognize the value of shorter races. Many marathons now offer half-marathon*

options. Stand-alone halves have increased in popularity. More and more new runners have begun to take the sensible approach of scheduling a half-marathon as their first race and later tackling a full as seasoned veterans.

Most of us grumpy coaches endorse that approach, but we also hope that your first marathon is not your last running race at any distance. This is because 5K and 10K races also can be fun. You don't want to leave the sauce off your pasta, do you?

For Your Consideration

- Racing satisfies the very human need for competition: It sharpens us on many levels and makes us stronger.
- Racing can serve as a substitute for regular track workouts if you don't like the confined feeling of a track.
- Racing is a good test of fitness levels.
- Racing is a good way to promote the social aspect of running.
- Don't overdo it—take one easy day for each mile raced.
- Even a race gone bad is an educational experience, and an incentive to learn to do better at the next race.
- In your self-tests, go down to distances as short as 400 meters.
- Look for all-comers meets where you can race at shorter distances against other runners. Competing against other runners is usually good for a 4 to 5 percent increase in your speed.
- Although the 5K is the most popular road race distance these days, for a more accurate test of your performance leading into your next marathon, look for a 10K or one of the increasingly popular half-marathons.
- Fashion a longer (15- to 18-mile, or 24- to 29-kilometer) course that you can use on a regular basis to test your fitness as you count down toward your next longer road race. Keep careful records of your performance on that course so you can compare it to the time you are shooting for.

ESCHEW RACING

with

Dick Beardsley

At one of the board meetings of the Napa Valley Marathon last year, we were all given something of a start when Mark Bunger, a California Highway Patrol officer and board member, passed out a packaged wristband similar to the yellow Livestrong bands Lance Armstrong has been selling on behalf of cancer research. "I've got enough for all the runners' bags," he said.

Gard Leighton and I glanced at the 3-inch-square piece of literature packaged with the purple wristband, then at each other. The headline on the little square of paper shouted, "RACING KILLS!"

"Only once in a while," Gard muttered. Gard Leighton knows racing: As a masters runner, he earned a gold belt buckle at the Western States 100 by turning in 10 sub-24-hour performances.

It took Mark a moment to realize what Gard and I were reacting to. "Oh jeez," he said. "I never thought of that." The wristbands were designed to discourage streetcar racing, a growing menace among young people in California. The connotation for our marathon hadn't occurred to him.

Considering the total number of people taking part in running road races, the number of people who die during a race is infinitesimally small. In most cases, racing on a regular basis strengthens athletes by substantially exercising the heart, significantly expanding the lung capacity, raising the $\dot{V}O_2max$, raising the lactate threshold, increasing leg muscle strength, and increasing the ability to focus.

Racing a car blows out the carbon buildup, allowing the machine to better do what it does by doing it for a short time at its max. But you don't want to run a car too fast too often. You can see the results of too many jackrabbit starts by pulling up behind some young stud piloting a supertuned little Japanese import that leaves a light blue film of smoke in its wake. Too much pressure on the little engine is burning out the rings.

The same applies to a runner. Too much racing aggravates the slightest biomechanical defect until the offended body part screams for relief. Too many microscopic tears accumulate until, like droplets of mist on a car's windshield, they run into each other, creating ever-larger tears until they produce a serious injury. Too many racing miles and not enough easy miles also builds up a deficit of energy: The fuel tank is never allowed to refill itself.

Back in the late 1970s and early 1980s, the running clubs in the San Francisco Bay Area used to get together to select a Runner of the Year. One of the qualifications for being chosen Runner of the Year was a high number of points amassed for the number of miles raced during the previous year. To accumulate more points, some candidates would race three or four times in a weekend, which was easy enough to do in the Bay Area because a dozen races or more were available each weekend. Some of the people who won that award haven't run in more than a

decade. They did a marvelous job of burning themselves out physically, mentally, and spiritually—or of becoming chronically injured. They burned out the ole rings once too often.

The rule of thumb for training and racing is to allow one day of easy running for each mile of hard racing. Using that yardstick, you could safely race a 10K every weekend, or a marathon once a month.

Mark Twain used to refer to refilling his tanks after he wore himself out either writing or going on lecture tours. Anyone who has been around running for a long time, has raced on a regular basis, and has learned to listen to his or her body knows this simple fact: It takes a fair amount of time to refill the tanks on a physical level; it takes even longer to refill the tanks on a mental and psychological level; and it takes longest of all to refill the tanks on a spiritual level. (This concept will be periodically raised throughout this book.)

Let's take a look at each of the three tanks. Physically, racing hard makes great demands on a runner on a number of levels: It requires the expenditure of a great deal of energy, tears down muscle tissue, strains connecting tissue and ligaments, and beats up on literally every organ in the body, from the stomach to the bladder.

Of course, given adequate amounts of rest, the incredibly adaptive human machine comes back stronger than ever. The key phrase here is *adequate amounts of rest*. We can't continually tear down the body systems and expect them to continue to function well if they aren't allowed to recuperate. Racing too often at any distance places a barricade between the body's potential to heal and its ability to do so.

Fortunately, all it takes to come back stronger is a dedicated rest period—not unlike the two periods in a year that are provided by nature: the summer when it's too hot and the winter when it's too cold. Several very accomplished racers I know annually take an entire month off every year to allow their bodies to rest and to repair the microscopic tears and bruises that racing and high mileage can cause (see chapter 15).

What about the mental and psychological tank? Racing well and often requires a great deal of focus and dedication—dedication to the training needed to race well, and focus to apply that training to the race itself. This focus and dedication come on top of or in addition to the other aspects of life that require focus and dedication, such as family and friends, work requirements, volunteer efforts, and ongoing information accumulation and education.

Although there is a ready formula that can be applied to resting after racing (one easy day for each mile raced), there is no easy formula for refilling the mental and psychological tank. It would be nice to think that the seasons of the year provide an answer: that if we go easier during summer and winter, our mental and psychological tank will be

refilled, and we'll have a more successful spring or autumn. This may be true. Using the summer and winter as base-building seasons in which to increase weekly mileage in a gentle, relaxed manner may provide plenty of time to allow the mental and psychological tank to refill.

Unfortunately, not everyone takes the time to refresh and replenish. Many hard-core racers race as often as they can—until they either become injured or burned out, which is another way of emptying the mental/psychological tank. The more you extend your racing season, the longer you will need to come back from it. Certainly, we all know ultrarunners who race an ultra every weekend. They rationalize this by insisting that they don't run hard and it's usually on a soft surface. That's all well and good, but racing miles are racing miles. They add up. And they take a toll.

Racing too frequently or too long until you break down or burn out makes it more difficult to come back. Like a pump that must be primed when its tank is allowed to empty out completely, the body and mind that are raced dry will take an inordinate amount of time to make a legitimate comeback. If you come back too quickly after racing yourself into the ground physically and mentally, you significantly increase your chances of injury.

What about refilling the spiritual tank? That's the toughest of all. The spiritual tank is the most elemental. It is the tank from which your dedication to running draws its nourishment. It can become drained in the wake of incredibly difficult efforts, either too much racing or racing too hard. You may reach a point at which you let out a belabored sigh and sink to the ground, totally spent. From this perspective you gaze down the road and all you see is more road and it all seems to be just too much.

Some runners and racers never recover from spiritual exhaustion. This can happen to novice runners who want to run a marathon as their first race. Because their tanks are never filled to start with (because racers' tanks are filled by a drip process, not by a fire hose), once they have completed the marathon, they have no exhilarating and uplifting urge to continue running and racing. Their effort has exhausted them on too many levels to make a comeback or to want more, and the main reason is that they never eased themselves into the fray to start with.

Although this may seem like blasphemy to many racers, I suggest that your body, mind, and spirit will benefit from taking every fifth year of your running career as a retreat or recovery from racing. Take the year off from racing and just run for fun. Besides allowing time for all three tanks to refill to bursting, such a break would allow you to come back to racing with a fresh outlook and a tremendous reserve of energy.

Eschewing racing for a year would not be the end of your racing career. It might be just the opposite. Consider the timeworn saying: Absence

makes the heart grow fonder. This can apply to your racing, so that when you come back, your heart is totally refreshed.

Along the same line, don't attempt to run or race through injuries. Such painful efforts may seem heroic on some levels, but on other levels all you are doing is guaranteeing that your running or racing career will be finite.

One runner who knows injury and burnout from overracing is Dick Beardsley, famous as half of the duo (along with then world-record-holder Alberto Salazar) that staged the Duel in the Sun at the hot 1982 Boston Marathon. Both of them went under 2:09 on a day when such a performance seemed impossible.

Dick's life has been a roller-coaster. We often joke that if a thunderstorm comes up over the horizon, don't stand next to him, because the first lightning strike is bound to hit him. He went through a horrendous farming accident that nearly tore off his leg, he has been involved in several vehicular accidents, and he has undergone more operations than a lab rat.

I asked Dick to put into perspective the wisdom one gains after many years of running and racing when it comes time to admit that maybe racing right now isn't the best thing for you. This is what he wrote:

> *Racing is the reward you give yourself from all the hard training you put in, but can it lead to injury or burnout? Yes!*
>
> *Back in my younger, faster days, no one loved to race as much as I did, perhaps with the exception of Billy Rodgers. I would run 30 to 40 races a year, from 5K through the marathon, but that kind of excess can catch up to you!*
>
> *In 1981 I ran five marathons and over 30 other road races. I had another marathon scheduled but had to pull out after being attacked by dogs while I was out on a training run. By October of that year I no longer had the excitement of waking up every morning and going on my first training run of the day. I remember almost having to drag myself out of bed to run. I then ran the International Peace Race in Youngstown, Ohio (25K). I ran terribly and really thought I had lost it. As I look back, there is no doubt that I was suffering from burnout! I had trained so hard and raced so much without a break. It was no wonder my mind and body did not look forward to running anymore. I took the entire month of December off with no racing and running only five miles a day at a very easy pace. By the end of the month, I was raring to go!*
>
> *After the 1982 Boston Marathon, I was really beat up physically and mentally. I should have backed off my training, but I did not because I had committed to Grandma's Marathon 62 days after Boston. I was*

fortunate to win that race, but it was really difficult and I should have taken time off afterward, but I didn't. Instead I ran two 10Ks in Alaska the following week!

By August I was training for the New York City Marathon and my left Achilles' tendon started getting a little tight. No big deal, I thought. I continued to race, but my Achilles' tendons kept getting worse. The day before the NYC Marathon, I ran the last four miles of the course and was limping by the end because my Achilles' tendon was hurting so badly.

Did I withdraw from the race! No! I should have, but my thought at the time was, "This is such a big race, the adrenaline will take care of the pain." It didn't, and by the time I ran off the far side of the Verrazano-Narrows Bridge at two miles, my left Achilles' tendon was hurting so badly that it was affecting my right leg.

I should have dropped right there, but I kept hoping it would feel better. It didn't, and I finished well behind Alberto Salazar, the winner that day.

To make a long story short, I ended up having to have two surgeries on my Achilles' tendon to fix it. The moral of this story is: Racing is fun, it's a great way to incorporate speed work, competition makes you a better runner, and so on, but too much of a good thing can lead to burnout or injury. Please don't let that happen to you.

I learned my lesson. As recently as the March 2010 Napa Valley Marathon, I planned to run the first 13 miles as a workout. No way. By 11 miles I knew that to go any farther was to invite more injury. I dropped out and got a ride back to the finish area.

Throughout most of my running career, I have basically been saying, "Do what I say and not necessarily what I do." No more. I think that's called maturity. It just took me a while longer than most to grow up in that regard.

Take it from me: When you're injured or burned out, stop. You can never regain tomorrow what you foolishly waste today.

For Your Consideration

- Too many people who get involved in the racing side of running become so enamored with it that they regularly overdo it and invariably spend part of their year licking their wounds. Consider applying the rule of one easy day for each mile of racing.

- Not all racing has to be done at full race speed. For those who deal daily with an inbred competitive nature, this may sound ridiculous. "When I pin on a number, man, I'm going for it," they would probably say. However, you can experience all the excitement of a race by using it as a slightly harder training run.

- You can also consider using a shorter race as the middle portion of a longer workout. If you are scheduled for an 18-miler on Sunday, consider finding a half-marathon where you time it so that you jog two or three miles and get to the start just as the race goes off, racing the half at 85 percent. As soon as you're finished, jog another two or three miles as a cool-down.

- Many excellent racers take a whole month off each year to engage in nonimpact, casual sport activities. Others do nothing at all, giving their muscles the time and space to recuperate from all the microtears they endured during the racing season.

- Taking a whole year off from racing while still casually running will not be the end of your racing career. In fact, it might extend it for another four or five years, which is nearly as beneficial as if you were coming to the sport fresh and new.

TRAIN SPECIFICALLY

with

Mel Williams, PhD

You don't use a garden rake to collect mercury. You no longer go to a barber to have a tumor excised. You don't order liver and onions if you're a vegetarian.

I think Ben Franklin said all of those things. Maybe not.

What this subject of specificity boils down to is that to get significantly better at running and racing, you need to put in a great deal of effort practicing at the type of running and racing you are planning to do. The essence of specificity of training is summed up beautifully in comments from 2004 Olympic marathon bronze medalist Deena Kastor in an interview with Hal Higdon (*Marathon & Beyond* magazine, May/June 2008, p. 48):

> With every race, you try to train as specifically as possible. If you are running cross-country, you want to train on some grass and hills, and if you're getting ready for a marathon, you want to make sure you are on the roads, slapping the pavement for a good part of your weekly mileage. If running track, you want to do some sessions on the track. It's always the specificity of training no matter what the event.

Beautifully said.

As we've discussed before in this book, the human body, unlike a robot, is infinitely adaptable. It's more like one of those transformer things: able to adjust shape and function—if given sufficient time to do so.

Consider, for example, that historically good cross-country runners translate into good marathon runners. Bill Rodgers placed well in the World Cross-Country Championships before he burst onto the scene as a winner at Boston and New York. Same with Grete Waitz, who repeatedly won the World Cross-Country Championships. Same with Carlos Lopes, who twice won the World Cross-Country Championships (nine years apart, no less) and later won the gold medal in the Olympic marathon in 1984—at age 37, setting an Olympic record in the process.

Cross-country running and marathoning have a lot in common, but one thing that is not common between them and that has to be specifically trained for is pavement. The typical cross-country course puts the runner through a wide range of muscle stretches and contractions as the runner adapts to the rolling terrain; on a larger and longer scale, this is not atypical of a challenging marathon course (such as Boston). Cross-country courses typically have a number of hills (which build leg strength), as do many marathon courses (again, Boston).

What the two events don't have in common is the running surface. Cross-country is run on soft surfaces (grass, dirt, sometimes gravel). Marathons (excluding trail marathons) are run on asphalt or concrete. To adapt to the hard surfaces of marathons, runners must drag their bodies

out onto the paved roads and put their legs, ankles, and feet through a good deal of pounding to avoid injury. Moving directly from the soft cross-country surface to the hard road racing surface is a sure way to produce an injury. But feed the legs a gradual, gentle mix, increasing the hard surface gradually, and the body adapts.

A marathon runner who wants to run cross-country or trail ultras must increase mileage on the softer surface while also training eye–foot coordination. The runner must practice looking ahead a half-dozen foot plants to anticipate where and at what angle to plant the foot. The brain needs to practice analyzing upcoming foot plants and salting them away for automatic implementation. It is very difficult for most runners to simply step from the pavement to the trail without practicing that next-foot-plant anticipation polka.

Then there are the matters of volume, hills, and speed. When it comes to specificity of training loads, these things are another matter.

As Arthur Lydiard proved a half-century ago, one starts by building an ambitious aerobic base whether you are running 800 meters on the track or the Western States 100 Endurance Run. The aerobic base is the foundation. The roof (speed) and the walls (hills) are added only after the foundation (aerobic base) has been poured and allowed to set.

But once the aerobic base is set, the training that follows is heavy on specificity.

Strength is best built by regularly running hills. In a typical marathon training program, there are two approaches to building strength through the use of hills:

1. Run hills pretty much year-round so they are a standard fixture of your program. This approach is typical of runners who do a lot of trail ultras.

2. Dial a program of regular hill running into your program for 8 to 12 weeks before your marathon to increase leg strength that will help carry you through the final 10K of the marathon while those around you begin to falter.

Following are four specific methods for increasing speed:

1. Use the Frank Shorter method. Frank goes to the track twice a week year-round to maintain his leg speed.

2. Begin incorporating speed workouts at the track on a regular basis (e.g., once or twice a week) once your aerobic foundation is laid—say, 12 to 14 weeks out from your goal race.

3. Race at shorter distances on a regular basis. This method was used quite successfully by American distance runners back in the 1960s,

and explains their success at longer distances in spite of the fact that they went to the track only occasionally.

4. Combine methods 3 and 4: Do speed workouts at the track once a week, and for the second speed workout, go to a race over the weekend that is shorter than your goal race. This allows you to build leg speed that will be faster than you will need at your goal race. Remember that you can't expect your body to run six-minute miles in a 10K race if your body hasn't run six-minute miles (and faster) in practice. That's the other side of specificity: Practice specifically what you hope to translate to your races.

How about the matter of specificity when you incorporate cross-training into your training? Cross-training (pool running, cross-country skiing, bicycling, and any number of workouts on the wide variety of gym equipment at health clubs) should only be used as a substitute for a regular program of running when you are injured and cannot take the pounding on the roads. This is both because the cross-training (let's use bicycling as an example) is not training you specifically for your sport and because there is not a one-to-one fitness benefit between bicycling and running.

If you want to run well, train specifically to run. If you want to bicycle well, bicycle almost exclusively. It sounds incredibly simple: If you are hoping to play the oboe well, don't waste time practicing on the guitar.

This is not to say that cross-training has no benefit other than as a substitute activity when you are injured. Cross-training in another aerobic sport can maintain or even increase your aerobic fitness level, but running in a pool won't make you a better trail runner.

You need to run more to run better. You need to decide exactly what kind of running you want to excel in, and then train specifically for that type of running. This is certainly not to say that you can't train well for several types of running and racing. It is just unlikely that you can specialize in several types of running and racing at the same time. For everything there is a season.

To get a better appreciation of specificity from a purely scientific standpoint, I asked Mel Williams, PhD, founder of the department of human movement science at Old Dominion University at Norfolk, Virginia, and a frequent age-group winner at the Boston Marathon, if he could expand on it for us. He calls this specificity of training for distance runners:

Runners at all levels of competition want to know how to run a faster race. My research focus over the past 40 years has involved the study of ergogenic aids, also known as performance-enhancing substances and strategies, and sport performance. In my presentation to runners at

various race events, I note that several safe and legal ergogenic aids may enhance running performance, such as losing excess body fat, wearing lightweight racing flats, and consuming relatively small amounts of caffeine. However, I always note that proper training is the most effective means to improve race performance.

Hans Selye, the renowned Canadian endocrinologist, developed the concept of the general adaptation syndrome to explain health effects related to how the body reacts and eventually adapts to various types of stress, and his concepts have been adapted by scientists in other disciplines.

For example, exercise physiologists have discovered that body tissues, organs, and systems adapt in specific ways depending on the type of exercise stress imposed on them. Based on this research, they have coined the term specific adaptations to imposed demands, which is also known as the SAID principle. Specificity of training for distance running is based on the SAID principle.

There are several variations of specificity of training for sport performance. For example, many runners today engage in cross-training, and many participate in multiple-sport events, such as the triathlon. Specificity of training is obvious for triathletes because they must train not only for running, but also for swimming and cycling, which not only are different sport skills but also use different muscle groups. To improve in swimming, you must swim. To improve in cycling, you must cycle. To improve in running, you must run.

As a distance runner, you must optimize a number of physiological functions to enhance your performance. In general, proper training will help induce the following adaptations to help increase your aerobic capacity, or the ability to consume and use oxygen to produce energy, which is the primary metabolic process involved in endurance sports.

- *Increased blood volume*
- *Increased capacity of the heart to pump more blood per beat*
- *Increased diffusion of oxygen from the lungs into the blood*
- *Increased oxygen-carrying capacity of the blood*
- *Increased oxygen uptake by the active muscles*
- *Increased number and size of mitochondria in muscle cells, which increases their ability to produce energy from oxygen*
- *Increased lactate threshold, which increases the running speed at which the muscles begin to rely increasingly on anaerobic energy production*
- *Increased running economy or running efficiency*

Proper training programs will help optimize these physiological adaptations and, concomitantly, may also enhance psychological and biomechanical adaptations important to distance running performance.

At one time, long, easy running was the major focus of distance runners. However, in the late 1940s a young Czechoslovakian runner, Emil Zatopek, helped pioneer changes in training strategies for distance runners. The self-coached Zatopek would often engage in very fast interval running, such as forty 400-meter repeats. When asked by other runners why he trained at such a fast pace, Emil's response was, "Why should I practice running slow? I already know how to run slow. I must learn how to run fast." Zatopek went on to earn three gold medals at the 1952 Helsinki Olympic Games—in the 5,000 and 10,000 meters as well as the marathon. He is recognized as one of the greatest runners of all time and one of the pioneers in revolutionizing training for distance runners.

Running fast is now an integral component of the distance runner's training regimen. In my opinion, as an exercise physiologist and distance runner, one of the best books on the science of distance running training is Daniels' Running Formula, *now in its second edition, by Dr. Jack Daniels. Dr. Daniels explains the purpose of training at various running speeds. In brief, the following represent the purposes of training at varying running speeds of increasing velocity:*

- *Easy pace running promotes desirable muscle cell changes and develops the cardiovascular system: the heart, lung, and blood vessels.*

- *Marathon pace running provides specific race pace conditions for marathon runners, and is an alternative to easy pace running for others.*

- *Threshold pace training is used to improve endurance by increasing the lactate threshold, the point at which the runner begins to accumulate lactic acid that may contribute to fatigue.*

- *Interval training is fast running designed to increase maximal oxygen uptake.*

- *Repetition running is faster than interval training and is designed to improve speed and running economy.*

Dr. Daniels' book provides an individualized training program based on one's current running performance, and provides recommended workouts for each specific type of training. Optimizing all facets of oxygen consumption, utilization, and economy is the key to maximizing distance running performance.

Specificity of training also applies to specific race conditions. One consideration may be a race course with challenging hills. In such cases, training on hills of similar grades and lengths for several months will help improve hill-running performance by stressing specific muscle groups. Training should incorporate not only uphill runs, but downhill runs at race pace as well. Running downhill during training will help develop the ability of active muscles to minimize small muscle tears, the main cause of muscle soreness.

Additionally, specificity of training applies to environmental conditions, particularly increased heat and humidity. When the environmental heat stress increases, reduce your training intensity or duration. Over time, gradually increase your training distance and intensity while you undergo the process of acclimatization. Your body systems make some specific adaptations as you acclimatize to running in conditions of high heat stress. For example, if you are already trained, 10 to 14 days of training in the heat may induce the following adaptations:

- *You may increase your blood volume by 5 to 10 percent or more.*
- *You will increase your sweat production.*
- *You will lose less sodium in your sweat.*

All of these adaptations may help you run more efficiently under warm race conditions by decreasing your core temperature and reducing your heart rate.

There may be other issues dealing with specificity of training. For example, if a specific sport drink will be served during a marathon, you might want to use that sport drink in your training. If you are to run a race at high altitude, some altitude training may provide some beneficial acclimatization effects.

Overall, an individualized program based on the specificity of training principle is the most effective means for an athlete to optimize his or her genetic potential.

For Your Consideration

- Decide what type of running and racing you wish to specialize in (cross-country, trail ultras, road marathons and halfs, indoor track), and then train to that type of running.
- To do well in any type of running and racing, always start by building a solid aerobic base.
- Incorporate hill workouts to add leg strength and to become better at running hills—both uphill and down.

- Don't overdo speed workouts, but once you have built your aerobic base, begin to add speed either by going to a track or by entering shorter races—or by doing both.
- Cross-training can be a valuable complement to your regular running, but is never a straight-across, one-for-one substitute.

AP Photo

DON'T IGNORE OTHER BODY PARTS

with

Joan Benoit-Samuelson

Although you can develop tremendous cardiovascular fitness from doing nothing but running, other parts of your body deserve some attention, too, if for no other reason than to bring your body closer to a place of balance. In the process, you will be contributing to the longevity of your running and fitness.

Aerobic sport and fitness activities that rely primarily on the legs get the job done as well as they do because the legs contain the largest bones and muscles in the body. As such, they contribute a lot in a minimum amount of time compared to other body parts.

However, using the analogy of the automobile, the best- and longest-running cars are those that have been cared for from bumper to bumper, are regularly serviced, and have correct alignment.

Runners are notorious for strong legs and sticklike arms. Look at a photo of a world-class runner. Chances are you'll see superb muscle definition in the legs and arms that look as though they'd be hard-pressed to heft a jelly donut.

Many years ago, when a bevy of runners from our office used to go to the local gym over lunch hour, we'd occasionally challenge one of the bodybuilders to a contest on the leg-thrust machine. Although the runner usually weighed about half what the bodybuilder did, they were pretty even as far as how much weight they could raise by thrusting their legs forward. And the runner could usually beat the bodybuilder in the number of repetitions. But lure the runner over to the chin-up bar, and it was a disaster. Although light in body weight, the runner could seldom do more than one chin-up.

It wasn't that way, though, for the triathletes who frequented the gym. Because of long hours using their arms in the swimming pool and many miles and hours of wrestling the handlebars of their bikes, the triathletes were usually very well balanced as far as their muscle development went on both the lower and upper body. They had no trouble doing chin-ups.

The bodybuilders, for their part, were not all evenly proportioned. Some of them failed miserably when they entered bodybuilding contests because they spent way too much time on the chest and arms and ignored most of the rest of the body.

For the runner who wants to be at it for the long run, who wants to have a body that is reasonably balanced and therefore not prone to injuries because of muscular imbalances, a nominal amount of time and energy spent on developing some aspects of the upper body would be well spent. And no, we're not taking a cue from certain running magazines that insist that runners need six-pack abs, although some attention to developing decent abdominal muscles would go a long way toward keeping a vertical torso in the latter stages of a race, particularly the marathon, when most runners tend to droop.

Unlike sprinters, who tend to develop more muscle mass because of their need for explosive muscle reaction, distance runners need to make themselves strong while keeping their bodies as light as is practical. There is a definite cost to carrying extra muscle mass over the long miles of training and racing.

A well-toned runner is a better—and stronger—runner.

If you are a distance runner, you can improve upper-body function and endurance by regularly (three to five times a week) doing a mere four exercises. You can easily do these in the comfort of your own home, and for zero dollars.

The four simple exercises are the sit-up, push-up, basic arm curl, and chest opener.

Everyone knows what a sit-up is, and the same is true of the push-up. The arm curl and chest opener are equally simple, but they require some sort of weight to make them work more easily. As someone who likes to keep life as simple as is practical, the weight I use for the latter two exercises is a sturdy piece of firewood. You could just as easily use hand weights. Or, if you commit to doing enough repetitions, no weights at all. (To appreciate using no weights at all, raise your arms above your head 100 times. By 50 reps you'll get the idea that gravity is a serious force in our lives.)

A sit-up should be done using a limited range of motion so as not to injure the lower back. Because every set of muscles in the body has a corresponding set of opposing muscles, when we develop the abdominal muscles by doing sit-ups, we help the opposing set of muscles in the lower back. To do a good sit-up, find a piece of heavy furniture. Lie down on your back in front of it. Slip your toes under the front of the furniture to anchor yourself. Bend your knees to a 90-degree angle and cross your arms over your chest. Using your abdominal muscles, raise your torso off the floor but only to 45 degrees; anything beyond that threatens to pull your back muscles and could cause injury.

Many people can do a sit-up without anchoring their feet. I find it almost impossible to do a proper sit-up without being anchored, either with my toes under a piece of furniture or with a spotter holding down my ankles.

A basic push-up comes in two models: standard and modified. The standard push-up is extremely simple. Lie down on the floor on your abdomen, keep your legs together, and place your hands palm-down on the floor under your shoulders. Using your toes as the hinge point and keeping your body straight, push yourself up off the floor using your arms. When your arms go straight, pause for a count, and then lower yourself.

The modified push-up is for those who lack strength in their arms. For the modified push-up, use your knees as the hinge point instead of your

toes. Do the push-up as you normally would. By using the knees as the hinge point, you are removing the lower part of your body's weight from the equation, thereby making it much easier to pull this off. Once you can do 20 modified push-ups easily, change over to standard push-ups, but at a lower volume—perhaps five to eight.

Arm curls are extremely simple. Stand straight and tall and hold the piece of firewood or another weighted object in your hands in front of your hips. Now, while keeping your upper arms perpendicular to the floor, slowly curl your forearms up toward your chest. Pause for a count, and then lower.

Chest openers are simply a more complex version of arm curls. Begin the exercise as you would an arm curl. Bring your piece of firewood or some other weight up to your chest while keeping your upper arms perpendicular to the floor. Pause at your chest for one count, and then slowly raise the weight above your head, using both your upper and lower arms, and pause there for a count of one. Then, keeping your upper arms perpendicular to the floor, lower the firewood or weight behind your head to your neck, pausing there for a count. Reverse the process, pausing at each of the junctures you paused at before.

None of these four exercises will bulk up your muscles. Taken together, they will help build up your abdominals and your arms, while also contributing to opening up your chest.

How many should you do to start? Start with 10 sit-ups, 5 push-ups, 20 arm curls, and 20 chest openers. Gradually, as the exercises become more comfortable, add a few more to each session. Once you can do 50 sit-ups, 25 push-ups, 100 arm curls, and 100 chest openers, stay at that level. That's plenty.

Next, you hear a lot of discussion about cross-training among runners. Cross-training is certainly a good way to add some variety to your training, but use cross-training (bicycling, swimming, pool running, cross-country skiing, and winter biathlon) workouts to supplement your running, not to replace it. As discussed in chapter 7 (Train Specifically), you learn to run better by running.

Bicycling is a good way to supplement running and to save your legs and feet from pounding the pavement once or twice a week, although you need to do about four miles of cycling to equal one of running. Moreover, for cycling to be effective, you need to be pedaling constantly. Another advantage of cycling is that it works your knees through a wider range of motion; as a result, when you get off the bike and run, you enjoy a higher knee lift and typically a stronger stride.

Then there's the matter of stretching: to do it or not to do it. I've never been a big proponent of stretching. I can cite a lot of good runners who are adamantly opposed to stretching. They believe that it undoes some

of what they do their running for: to make certain muscles toned and powerful. Stretching, they believe, makes the muscles way too pliable and in the process defeats the purpose of running to train your body to run.

Of course, at the other end of the spectrum are those who are huge proponents of the miraculous results of stretching. Their contention is that you need to stretch an overworked muscle to loosen it, and you need to stretch to prevent injuries. Unfortunately, some studies have indicated that one of the most common causes of running injuries is stretching.

I can certainly see that point, especially when I watch people at the start of a race on a cold morning at 6:00 a.m., their poor bodies just recently forced out of a nice, warm bed, sitting on the hard, cold roadway stretching. I cringe when I see that, picturing the poor, cold, stiff muscle fibers being ripped apart, crying out for mercy.

If you are going to stretch, do so *after* you're done running. The running will have warmed up and loosened up the muscles so they will be much more willing to give a little instead of being torn apart.

Famed New Zealand coach Arthur Lydiard made the observation that you don't see impalas stretch before they attempt to outrun the lions.

What's the most important muscle that needs regular exercising? Right: the brain. Regular aerobic exercising nourishes the brain with fresh imports of oxygen and nutrients that help it flourish. Use the brain, too, to think through your exercise program and to map out one that will fit your lifestyle and the time you have available. A lot of runners these days seem to run without engaging their brains; they actually turn them off by turning on loud music. Running, like sailing, is a cerebral sport. Like the captain of a sailboat, your brain should be directing all the various parts of your body in their duties during the process of running, as well as monitoring the strength or fatigue levels of those body parts. It's terrific to run with your heart (which, of course, also benefits greatly from aerobic exercise), but running with your head will keep you running longer and safer.

Someone who heartily believes in nourishing all aspects of the human being is Joan Benoit-Samuelson, winner of the first-ever (1984) women's Olympic marathon. Living in Maine, Joanie benefits from cross-training in the winter by being an avid cross-country skier.

She is also an advocate of pool running. In 1984 it looked as though she would be unable to make the U.S. Olympic Marathon Trials because of knee surgery. But by doing vigorous pool running to maintain her fitness level, she won not only the Trials in Olympia, Washington, but also the Olympic marathon.

She agreed to share some of her beliefs about getting the whole person fit:

I call this little essay "Cross My Heart and Hope to Train for Years to Come." I write this with the hope of giving you some compelling insights and reasons for incorporating cross-training into your regular running routine.

Having long been an advocate for balance in one's life, and understanding the significance of the mind, body, and spirit triad referenced by many physical education and activity professionals, I have tried to balance these three subjects in my own life both on and off the roads where I do most of my training. Having logged over 125,000 miles (201,168 km) during my career, I have had plenty of time to think about all sorts of topics that relate to my active lifestyle. Perhaps this is credential enough to share lessons learned while thinking on the run. Just the simple acts of running and thinking cover the mind and body. The spirit part comes in the passion that keeps me going.

While constantly trying to maintain balance in my life as it relates to family matters, training, travel, community responsibilities, and the unexpected request or engagement, I find that my mind, body, and spirit are constantly exercised on a daily basis even though no two days in my life seem to be the same. Yes, it is true that I don't have a given job description, but I can assure you that I'm never bored. However, it is the desire to find balance in training for road racing and running in general that warrants attention in this book.

It seems as though running is the basis for all activity, no matter what that activity may be. If we are attempting to achieve certain goals in the sport of running, we need to run with some form of rhyme and reason. If we are performing a certain task and all of a sudden realize that we have something baking in the oven, we need to run to the oven to prevent the item from burning. If we find ourselves behind schedule for an important meeting, flight, or appointment, we often run to the designated location. Essentially, we can run for a variety of reasons throughout the day, and the variety of obligations during our days gives us balance. We need to run for balance, and we need to balance our running.

Runners are notorious for not dealing well with injuries. I'm willing to bet that, more times than not, runners become injured because they don't balance their training very well. They believe they must put in as many miles as possible to achieve optimal success in the sport. I used to think this was true—until injuries finally got the best of my thinking and I saw the benefits of cross-training.

In my first book, Running Tide, *I mention the importance of the four distinct seasons in Maine as they relate to building different physical strengths. During my childhood we would build snow sculptures in the winter, garden in the spring, build sand castles at the beach in the*

summer, and rake leaves in the fall. Little did I know it at the time, but I was working on developing different physical strengths well before I knew what the sport of running and injuries were all about. Today, as an aging athlete in the sport, I know all too well about injuries.

To avoid injuries, I try to balance my interests with my training. Fortunately, many of my interests relate to physical activity so I can call pursuit of these burning interests cross-training. The same way the seasons provide a palette for our year, an array of physical activities can fulfill us in body, mind, and spirit.

For Your Consideration

- Don't allow your running to exclude other physical activities that can benefit the rest of your body.

- Set aside some time, perhaps just before bedtime, to do the four basic muscle-building upper-body workouts.

- If you decide to incorporate a stretching routine as part of your running and fitness plan, learn to stretch properly from someone who knows how to do it to avoid injury. A long-running classic book on the subject is simply titled *Stretching* by Bob Anderson.

- Use the basic aerobic fitness you've developed from running to enjoy other aerobic sports, but don't overdo it. Too much of another aerobic sport can injure or tighten muscles that you aren't used to exercising at an extreme level.

- You don't need to join a gym to develop strength and endurance in muscles that you don't normally use in running. And you don't need to buy expensive equipment. Be creative with using household items as your gym equipment. Decades ago Jack LaLanne, the eternal fitness guru, learned how to keep himself fit while on the road by making use of the furniture in a hotel room. If you keep it simple enough, you can do your auxiliary exercising just about anywhere.

RUN WITH A PLAN

Repeat the same action too often and both you and the thing you are doing become stale and mundane. Sounds like a perfect description of just about any manufacturing job or any dead-end office job. It can also be a description of a monotonous running program and a perfect formula for giving up running entirely.

My high school science teacher had been teaching the same science lessons for so long that he had to use those reinforcement things on the holes of the papers in his three-ring binder. We sneaked a look at his plant biology binder one afternoon and found out that he even had his timeworn jokes written in the margins.

Running long distances is a repetitive activity if there ever was one. Put one leg in front of the other, alternate, repeat. What saves running from being entirely monotonous is that it offers infinite variations. Once warmed up, we can meld with the run until it becomes autonomic; we typically do the training in a hard/easy manner so we aren't doing exactly the same workout every day; and, if we are smart, we periodize our training and racing, coming at it in waves, or cycles.

Periodization is often compared to the seasons of the year. In other words, for everything there is a season. Over the past several years, among truly hard-core coaches, we have seen the concept of periodization get whittled down, redefined, expanded, reexamined, and doused with arcane definitions that no average runner could ever understand. It's even been broken into linear and nonlinear periodization. The concept has been further confused by the hatching of new meanings for *cycle* and *wave,* as though they were totally separate from building periods, as though they were fields in which a specific series of workouts will lead to a specific harvest.

There is no need for the average runner to grow a headache over trying to understand the concept of periodization. In fact, maybe the easiest way to come at periodization is from the back door, by asking, What *isn't* periodization?

What isn't periodization is running in California, where for literally the entire year you can pretty much keep your running going forward . . . until you injure yourself from training too much and too long. Allow me to use my own stupid self as a bad example, an example of how not to train.

I began getting back into running in Alexandria, Virginia, in the early summer of 1977. The entire D.C. basin becomes extremely hot and humid over the summer and makes quality training difficult to come by. On the last day of July, I moved to Northern California to go to work at *Runner's World*. The weather was ideal. I quickly increased my mileage, and by the following April had run my first marathon. By the end of the year, I'd run eight marathons and several ultras, and I had

no intention of stopping because I was running well and the weather, although colder, was very cooperative. By February I had developed a sharp pain in the connecting tissue between my right calf and my Achilles' tendon. It felt like someone was inserting an ice pick. I backed off, and the injury healed. The following year I kept training, and again the same thing happened; but this time it was on the left leg. Next year, same thing, but it was back on the right leg.

Eventually, the weather genes I was born with in Pennsylvania kicked in, and I realized that nature doesn't want us to run hard all 12 months. By backing way down after my October marathon, my times improved, and I never had an injury between the calf and the Achilles' tendon again.

This is the negative way of looking at it: being forced by nature (as a result of my own stupidity and arrogance) to take a rest. To turn it around, you can ask, What kind of periods of building and sharpening can I schedule for the year to most effectively achieve my running goals for that year? What that does, in essence and in fact, is put you in charge of your own running fate.

Let's create our own definition of *periodization:*

> **Periodization:** The process of designating various periods throughout a year for building and then sharpening one's fitness to run and race at one's best, followed by periods of diminished racing and training to recover.

As you can see, the periods infer a beginning, a middle, and an end—at which point you begin to radically cut back both the quality and volume of running. But just because that wall at the far end of the designated period is inferred doesn't mean that we are apt to respect it. Most runners simply ignore the wall on the right side of a period laid out on a calendar and slide right into the next period . . . usually with disastrous results.

Let's break it down with an example. You want to run two quality marathons next year. You've done research and discovered that all the really good marathoners confirm that the human body can handle only two *quality* marathons in a 12-month period. Notice that we're using the word *quality.* That does not mean that you can't use additional marathons as long workouts if you are so inclined.

So, two quality marathons. When does nature dictate those marathons should be run? Spring and fall. Marathon calendars have disproportionate lumps of marathons in spring and fall because the weather is favorably inclined toward marathoning.

It typically takes 16 to 18 weeks of training to get ready for a marathon. Let's be generous with ourselves and use 18 weeks. Eighteen weeks times two (two marathons this year) equals 36 weeks committed to marathon

training and racing. This leaves 16 weeks for resting or easy running, eight weeks after each of the two marathon training sessions.

Within the 18 weeks of marathon training, we have the aerobic buildup (or base) period (say, 10 weeks), followed by six weeks of speed and hill workouts, followed by two weeks of tapering. The six weeks of speed would also include running hard in races shorter than the marathon. After the marathon, you can back off for eight weeks before beginning to rebuild your base.

If you want to do a fall cross-country program and a summer track program, the periodization training for these races is similar. You'll be able to hold a peak longer, though, because the cross-country and track races are significantly shorter than a marathon. Using the formula of one day of easy running for each day you race, you could be racing an 8K cross-country course once a week, and in summer, you could be running mile races at the track several times a week. But again, you want to dial in the eight weeks of easy running at the end of the season to allow your body to heal before beginning to build again.

I use the marathon as an example because the 18-week training period is an easily observed chunk of time marked on the annual calendar. The same periodization concept applies to shorter distances, although not the shorter-distance races you might plug into your 18-week marathon training program to use as sharpening and speed-building tools.

Most adult track seasons occur over the summer months (as opposed to high school and college track seasons). If you are a miler and have built up a base during the spring months and, coming into early summer, you used some shorter races to generate leg speed and build toward a midsummer peak, you can race several quality mile races each week for much of the summer before you peak. You'll still have some quality miles on the far side of your peak before (wisely) backing off on your racing—no matter how good it is going—toward a late-summer/ early autumn trough so you can begin recovering. A similar period is available if you are into doing shorter road races (5K and 10K), even if, like the July 4th Peachtree 10K in Atlanta, they are in the middle of the summer heat.

Because it is safe to race miles in proportion to easy days (i.e., one easy day for each mile raced), you can throw together a two-month period in which you race at various shorter distances (assuming you put in the base miles leading into your racing binge). So as not to lock yourself into one distance only, I refer to theses various shorter-distance races as "flights" of races, in that they are a mix. According to the *New Oxford American Dictionary*, it falls under this definition of *flight:* "a group of creatures or objects flying together, in particular: a flock or large body of birds or insects in the air, a group of aircraft operating together, esp.

an air force unit of about six aircraft." (I glommed onto this concept of flights by spending way too much time as a kid watching World War II documentaries in which the skies were filled with Allied aircraft of all shapes and sizes flying together on a shared mission, heading off to do damage to the evil Nazis.)

In running, a flight of races refers to a bunch of different distances that go nowhere near a marathon, all run in a two- or three-month period: maybe a 10K one weekend, followed by a 1-mile and a 2-mile run the next weekend at an all-comers' meet, followed by a 5K the next weekend, another 5K the weekend after that, a 7.6-mile (12.2 km) trail run the next weekend, and so on, until you've run out of calendar for that season. Then you should bag it for a couple of months to rest your weary body before again ramping up for another flight of races at the opposite end of the calendar.

Of course, to sample the whole dish of mixed nuts, the ideal would be to come off the winter season primed for a two-and-a-half-month spring flight of shorter races, followed by a backing off in the heat of the summer. During the summer, you could gradually begin building toward a fall marathon because the greatest variety and choice of marathons comes in the fall. Then it's time to back off for the annual winter down period. That schedule saves you the discomfort of having to build up too much mileage for too long a period in the foul winter months.

If you want it all, nothing is more widespread, all-inclusive, and complementary than racing from the mile to the marathon (including everything in between) all in one calendar year. You can also dial in shorter periods and can even use the eight weeks of easy running over the winter to dial in some alternate aerobic sport. In cold winter climates, runners often change over to cross-country skiing and biathlon races during the down period because cross-country skiing is so much gentler on the legs, ankles, and feet.

At the end of your fall racing season, buy a calendar for the next year and take an afternoon to sit down and design your periods of rest and work aimed at reaching your running and racing goals the next year.

For Your Consideration

- Save yourself a lot of forced downtime and injury by scheduling your running and racing seasons based on specific periods.
- Map out just what kind of racing you want to do for the next calendar year, and fashion in the buildup and sharpening you'll need to accomplish your goals.
- Never run more than two high-quality marathons in one year.

- Make good use of rest or easy running periods to heal microscopic tears in your muscles.
- Consider expanding your running by taking on several radically different kinds of racing in one calendar year, such as cross-country in the fall and a marathon in the spring.

AP Photo

RUN BY FEEL

In the movie *Body Heat*, the Ted Danson character takes off on a run when the urge strikes him. He doesn't change into fancy or trendy running gear. He just heads out wearing what he's wearing, and he comes back all sweaty. (Get it? Body heat. It's everywhere in this movie.) The first thing he does when he stops running is light up a cigarette. This is certainly a contrivance to set his character apart from the rest of the cast, and certainly not a training regimen most of us could get behind. But the Danson character *does* exemplify the concept of running by feel.

Any coach worth his or her salt would caution against simply running by feel. After all, there are proven ways to train to get certain results, ways that have been proven correct over and over for decades and through the massed results of hundreds of thousands of runners. Yet, if you are not obsessed with running a maximum of races or running races extremely well based on your talent, running by feel has a certain appeal. (As long as you don't interpret running by feel as "Hey, it's raining out there. I guess I don't feel like running today.")

Running or training by feel involves carefully reading your body to determine what kind of running it feels up to on a specific day. It sort of turns you into an organic heart-rate monitor: My body feels like a slow five-miler today. Or, my body seems up to a steady 20 this weekend.

Ah! you say. That goes against a lot of what this book supposedly teaches. You're both right and wrong. As you've probably noted, many of the chapters in this book are presented in opposing pairs: Do more mileage; no, no, do less. Go forth and do a bunch of races; no, no, stop racing. That kind of thing. This reflects a philosophy of dichotomy, sort of like the theory of working opposing muscles to make your body more balanced.

If you are a runner of duration, at times you will do best by doing one thing, and then other times you will serve yourself—and your running—best by doing just the opposite. To do the same thing over and over forever is to invite disaster, in the form of either boredom and burnout or persistent overuse injuries. Consider a variety of running stretched out over several years of your running career: this year training for the mile, next year training for the marathon, and the year after that doing no racing at all.

But getting back to running by feel: In many cultures of the world for a thousand or two thousand years BT (Before Telecommunications), communications were accomplished by men running great distances to deliver messages, often between a king and his lieutenants. In South America, runners chewed coca leaves to supplement endorphins so they could carry messages over high mountains between cities. In the Himalayan region, monk runners used chants to ameliorate discomfort as they carried messages hundreds of miles. In Hawaii the long-distance

Western Union runners were known as "the king's messengers." In the Greek city-states, the "all-day runners" were *hemerodromi*; they carried messages between city-states but were also military couriers (not too unlike the Aussie runners in the film *Gallipoli*).

Although we know that the hoplites of ancient Greece trained together to run wearing armor, we know little of the training of the hemerodromi, who were capable of running 150 miles in one direction to deliver a message. (We must keep in mind that the Greeks glorified sprinters in their culture; the hemerodromi were on the level in our society of bike messengers.)

We do know that the hemerodromi were awesome runners, in part from the writings of Greece's first historian, Herodotus. In his book *Histories*, he recorded this account of a messenger sent to drum up military support: "First, before they left the city, the generals sent off to Sparta a herald, one Pheidippides, who was by birth an Athenian, and by profession and practice a trained runner. . . . He reached Sparta on the very next day after quitting the city of Athens." We know that the distance between Athens and Sparta was 150 miles. Once he had his answer, Pheidippides turned around and ran back 150 miles to deliver the bad news of Sparta's inability to help. (Sparta, where the warrior breed was dominant, would have loved to come and join in the fun, but they were in the middle of a religious celebration and did not want to offend the gods.)

Unfortunately, Herodotus did not provide a sidebar in *Histories* explaining how Pheidippides and his comrades trained. We can assume that some of their training was in small groups (there were not a whole lot of them), although much of it would likely have involved long training runs alone, given that this was how they practiced their trade. They didn't run in pairs. They would have practiced running long, and they would have practiced how it best worked for them—that is, by feel.

In ancient Greece there were no human performance labs, no heart-rate monitors, no graduate students in physiology extracting muscle tissue from Pheidippides' calf to compare fast-twitch muscle fiber with slow-twitch. Running by feel was at the same time an art and a science. Pheidippides and his buddies learned by trial and error what worked. They knew when they ran to the edge of fatigue and when their running was fresh and filled with energy.

Unless you are incredibly prescient about your body, it takes some years of running before you intimately know the reaction to expect from your body in the wake of a specific workout. You might note that the last dozen times you ran hard at the track, you needed two rather than one day of easy running to recover. In bed first thing in the morning you might notice that your heart is still beating too hard and

too fast in its recovery mode to want to push it with a hard workout again today.

We can trace the intuitive training process down through the ages. Certainly the *pedestrians* of the 1870s had a real feel for what worked for them and what didn't. The professional pedestrians often took part in six-day races in venues such as Madison Square Garden, where they would compete before 25,000 spectators— most of them smokers and gamblers—for thousands of dollars in prize money. They were great experimenters. They walked and ran tremendous distances in training, so they had the miles on their feet, legs, and heart and they could literally *feel* the results of their intuitive training. Some of them walked for five hours straight wearing weighted boots; then took off the boots and ran for four or five additional miles, feeling the fleet-footedness after the drudgery of the previous lead-footed miles.

Because of the advanced feel they had for their training, 19th-century pedestrians were also expert about when to stop and when to skip a day. Edward Payson Weston was famous for knowing instinctively when to take a break so he could come back stronger. He did so several times during his famous 1861 walk from Boston to Washington, D.C., in the middle of winter.

In the early part of the 20th century, road race fields were small and consistently made up of a mix of blue-collar types who belonged to athletic clubs (often ethnic, such as the Irish athletic clubs in Boston) and college guys who liked to occasionally get away from the track. The clubs had coaches, but their influence over the club members was often tenuous at best and often limited to the club members who competed in what they considered the pure sports of track and field. There were small handbooks (often sold in conjunction with athletic equipment) that attempted to teach runners how to improve, but they were basic and very often dead wrong.

Adrian Lopez, one of my bosses in the mid-1970s, told me stories of his track days when he was at college at Notre Dame. He was a miler, but milers were trained to *never* run as far as a mile in training because it would exhaust them before the race. For this reason, they trained up to three-quarters of a mile and no more. Fortunately, we now know that is dead wrong. Adrian also said that road racers were looked down on by coaches as below contempt, as impure mutations of track runners.

Many of the road racers in the 1930s and 1940s shoe-horned workouts in around their day jobs and essentially trained by feel. If they felt their speed was lacking, they either entered another, shorter road race or ran a track race, of which there were many in those days.

Several Native Americans, specifically Tom Longboat (a Canadian) and "Tarzan" Brown, were reputed to train very much by feel—with

the expected result that sometimes their performances were outstanding and other times they were sorely disappointing. We now know, however, that for his Boston wins, Brown trained strenuously under the direction of a coach.

The great majority of road racers in the 1940s and 1950s lived in New England and on the West Coast, where there were plenty of road racing opportunities to satisfy them. Road racers were considered an odd lot, the bottom of the totem pole of runners. Or as Jock Semple, a road racer himself and later director of the Boston Marathon, called them, "ham and eggers."

A perfect example of the dichotomy between traditional training methods and training by feel was John J. Kelley, who won the Boston Marathon in 1957 running for the Boston Athletic Association, which by then was a mere shadow of its former glory. Kelley was also the AAU marathon champion eight years in a row. When he was a college student at Boston University, he wanted to run road races, but his college coach refused to allow him to do so. Therefore, he ran by feel on free days to build up mileage and became one of the best road racers in America, all behind his college coach's back.

In the 1970s, recent college graduates such as Frank Shorter and Bill Rodgers often stayed in touch with their college coaches to get training advice. More often, however, they exchanged training information within their running groups, because their college coaches knew little about road racing. Shorter and his friends lived and ran in the Gainesville, Florida, area, and Rodgers ran with the Greater Boston Track Club, which, ironically, specialized in the roads. Rodgers had the benefit of eventually falling under the guidance of eccentric and brilliant coach Billy Squires, but for years Rodgers was self-coached.

Within the past 20 years, runners have had the luxury of having coaches available (whether online, in clubs, or through the Team in Training program), but the large percentage of them don't train under coaches. They often wing it or jury-rig a training program from various sources to fit their own lifestyles.

Unless you are exceptionally sensitive to your body, training by feel does not deliver consistently good results in races, although it may provide longevity to a running program by avoiding anything that is too hard or painful. Of course, like many things in running, you can adapt almost anything to your benefit if you rely on the wisdom you have accumulated over the years to meld the two concepts: structural training and running as you feel.

If you are an experienced runner, you might hit a point in a training regimen in which you feel as though you are trashing your legs with too many hard workouts spaced too close together. Instead of proceeding

as planned, it might behoove you to go with your feel and back off the strict regimen for a few days and do easy runs that feel invigorating instead of injurious to your legs.

Consider the example of coach Bill Bowerman and one-time American marathon record-holder and author Kenny Moore. Bowerman intuited by watching Moore train that he would benefit by being taken out of the loop the rest of the team was in and given some extra-easy days each week. Moore benefited greatly from going easy on his legs after hard workouts. In that instance, Kenny Moore wasn't the one who had a good feel for what would work best for him; rather, his coach felt that Kenny would compete better by beating himself up less.

It is better to feel your way through some recovery days and then get back onto your program than to continue thrashing yourself because the program requires it and then be forced to back off for two weeks to recover properly. There is no law that says you can't be regimented and a feeling runner at the same time. It can work either way—or both ways at the same time.

If you are running for the simple joy of running (I tend to refer to it as Thoreau running), there is no better way to achieve satisfaction than to run by feel. It removes all stress and anticipation brought about by rigidly scheduled workouts. It is certainly a purer form of running.

What kind of practical tips could I give if you are such a runner—go thee forth and run? I can't say that because suppose you don't feel like running today? If you want to run by feel, you would do well to make heavy use of two devices: the heart-rate monitor and the journal. The journal can help you keep track of serendipitous successful training sequences arrived at by chance that actually produced good results, and the heart-rate monitor can help prevent overtraining, such as running too hard on an easy day because you're feeling good.

If you want to run by feel, more power to you. You have put yourself in the ranks of Pheidippides and Edward Payson Weston. Keep in mind, however, that you should never run to exhaustion. Always stop short of doing too much, simply because it takes about two weeks of easy running to come back to where you were the day before you went overboard.

Run by feel should certainly be the mantra for even the most meticulous runners when the downtime of the annual schedule comes along. After the racing season is over, allowing your body to dictate just what it wants to do and when (and even whether it wants to do anything) is a perfect way of allowing it to heal from an ambitious schedule. A good month of running how you feel around the holidays makes perfect sense, too. It returns you to a form of running that is as guilt-free and as natural as possible.

Of course, if you want to run by feel for the rest of your life, you're likely to run long and well.

For Your Consideration

- If you aren't shooting for a series of specific race results, there is no reason to not run by feel.
- During the off-season, running by feel is an excellent way to recover from the racing season.
- Even the most disciplined runner can benefit from a scheduled period of unscheduled running by feel.
- If you are a casual runner who runs by feel, there's no reason not to keep doing exactly what you're doing. You don't need to smoke a cigarette at the end of each run just to make yourself a more color-ful character. (I will refrain from telling you about Gary Cantrell, a director of ultra races, who smokes cigarettes.) The fact that you have reverted to running as many of our ancient ancestors did is colorful enough .

Photodisc/Getty Images

MOVE UP IN MILEAGE

A theory in long-distance running that was popular in the 1970s has reemerged as a mantra of successful world-class runners today: To become a better runner, run as much mileage as your body can stand for as long as practical, and then rest from your labors before restarting the cycle. This sounds so eminently logical and practical that it hardly seems worth saying. Yet, just as we have cycles in the seasons and cycles in a running career (think Lasse Viren peaking every four years in time for the 1972 and 1976 Olympics, where both times he won the 5,000 and 10,000 meters), we periodically need to state and then restate the obvious lest it be lost in the cacophony of scientific certainty and general interest know-it-all-ism.

What I mean is that logic doesn't always rest with the experts. In fact, on a fairly regular basis, the experts (in whatever field) bulldoze logic under a landfill of statistics and Swiss cheese research.

Let's look at a short history of running long to run best. In the first half of the 20th century, there was a fellow in New England named Clarence DeMar. He won the famed Boston Marathon seven times and arguably would have won it at least two or three more times if at the height of his prowess his doctors hadn't warned him to take time off from running to protect his enlarged heart (enlarged, as it turned out, by lots of aerobic exercise). Clarence, a reticent and often truculent man, used twice-a-day workouts to his advantage.

He wasn't a scientist who, after long and thorough study, came to the conclusion that twice-a-day workouts were the way to become a better marathoner. He was a printer who ran to and from work each day, a clean shirt tucked under his arm. He found that twice-a-day workouts fit well into his workday world; on weekends he ran longer distances. The mix allowed him to charge up a tremendous battery of strength and endurance, which served him well when he raced. It also allowed him to commute to and from work without having to pay for carfare. Clarence grew up poor, worked at a boys' home, and learned never to waste his money.

Other runners against whom Clarence competed began to take note of his racing success and began to adopt some of his training methods. Among those were John A. Kelley and John J. Kelley. John A. won Boston in 1935 and 1945 and earned a spot on the U.S. Olympic marathon team three times; John J. Kelley (no relation) won Boston in 1957, was an Olympic marathoner, and won the AAU Marathon Championships at Yonkers an incredible eight years in a row.

Between the two Kelleys, the legendary Czech distance runner Emil Zatopek set new standards for the *volume* of distance he trained per week to compete on the world stage. Zatopek remains the only runner in history to win the Olympic 5,000 meters, 10,000 meters, and the marathon in the same Olympic Games: 1952 at Helsinki.

In the 1960s New Zealand coach Arthur Lydiard codified the theory of long, slow distance as a base preparatory to specific strength and speed training not in a laboratory but in the Olympic record books by placing his neighborhood runners on the medals platform at the 1960 Olympic Games: Snell, gold in the 800 meters; Halberg, gold in the 5,000; and Magee, bronze in the marathon.

Also in the 1960s, Derek Clayton of Australia trained at mind-boggling volume and became the first marathoner to go under 2:11, 2:10, and 2:09. At one point there were rumors that Clayton was running 200 miles a week. I asked him about that in 1980. "I experimented with big mileage," he said, "but I never came near 200. But why should I have let on that I didn't? If runners I was racing against believed that and tried to do the same and ruined themselves, then that was all right with me."

By the time the 1970s arrived, American postcollegiate distance runners had concluded that a combination of heavy mileage, occasional speed training at the track, and a regular regimen of racing was a sorcerer's ambrosia for marathon success. At the 1972 Olympic Games in Munich, the U.S. marathon team placed first (Frank Shorter), fourth (Kenny Moore), and ninth (Jack Bachelor). No other national team before or since has ever placed so well in the Olympic marathon, not even the East Africans (Kenya and Ethiopia) in the modern era. It was a golden age for U.S. long-distance racing.

In the previous Olympics, the U.S. team (Moore, George Young, and Ron Daws) would have taken the team title if one existed. In the next Olympics after the 1972 extravaganza, Americans placed second (Shorter) and fourth (Don Kardong) and would have been first and third had winner Waldemar Cierpinski been disqualified for his use of performance-enhancing drugs. (When the Berlin Wall fell, the Stasi files were thrown open and Cierpinski's performance-enhancing drug regimen was exposed. Frank Shorter launched a campaign to strip Cierpinski of his gold and transfer it to himself, but the International Olympic Committee claimed it was all too far in the past to bother with.)

It was an intoxicating era for U.S. distance running. This period extended into the early 1980s when Americans Alberto Salazar and Dick Beardsley staged their historic Duel in the Sun at Boston in 1982. The top three places in Boston 1983 were taken by Americans (Greg Meyer, Ron Tabb, and Benji Durden), and in 1984 Joan Benoit-Samuelson won the first women's Olympic marathon in Los Angeles.

At that point, American distance running fell apart, in large part because the scientific community stepped in to assert that marathoners needed no more than 75 miles of training a week to perform at a world-class level. The extravagance of previous decades, in which marathoners were training regularly at 120 miles a week with experimental forays into

150 miles and even 200 miles a week, was belittled and denigrated by the scientists who studied running. Marathon running (and winning) was no longer to be an art form perpetrated by creative artists and coaches such as Arthur Lydiard, Ernst Van Aaken, Bob Sevene, Bill Squires, and others. It was to be dictated by slide rules and heart-rate monitors.

Within the past decade, distance coaches such as Bob Larsen, Joe Vigil, Al Salazar, Terrance Mahon, and others involved in regional U.S. distance-training enclaves have reinstituted longer long-distance training as a route to long-distance glory. The results were obvious at the 2004 Olympic Games in which Americans again medaled in both the men's and women's Olympic marathons, and the trend seems to be continuing with the development of outstanding distance runners such as Ryan Hall.

In an interview in *California Track & Running News* (January/February 2008, p. 36) in the wake of his astounding Trials win, Ryan Hall had this to say about distance: "I've been doing high mileage ever since day one. Mileage is nothing new to me. My legs respond better to it. For example, I've found that I can do really well for a 10K by putting in 120 miles a week. That's the kind of stuff I've been doing for my marathon training and that's when I feel my best. I've kind of found my niche."

But, you say, what do world-class distance runners doing megamile-age have to do with me? Excellent question. The answer is that it has *everything* to do with you improving both the efficiency of your training and the results of your racing.

"A high training volume improves many aspects of aerobic metabolism, including the number of red blood cells, hemoglobin concentration, muscle capillary and mitochondrial volumes, and aerobic enzymes, together resulting in greater oxygen-carrying capability and greater ability to use the available oxygen," concluded Jason Karp, PhD, in an article titled "Chasing Pheidippides" (*Marathon & Beyond*, May/June 2008, pp. 41-45).

Except for those on the verge of fatigue from too much mileage, every runner can benefit from adding a bit more mileage to the program. And in that tried-and-true but frustrating phenomenon, the runner who is already doing less will benefit much more from adding a little, whereas the runner who is doing most will need to do much more to gain minor advantages.

By gradually and carefully adding mileage, the average runner will gain on several fronts. The added mileage will increase the endurance reservoir and thereby increase performance, especially in the later stages of the marathon where mere mortals falter. The added mileage will also make the runner more efficient. To do anything well, we need to do it frequently and at some volume. But once we do, we naturally become more efficient at doing it. Everything from long-distance running to

playing chess to playing the piano or another musical instrument benefits from increasing the amount of practice we put in.

There is another benefit to becoming more efficient at running: The practice of running additional miles doesn't take as much additional time as you might think because you are typically getting better at it and therefore doing it at a faster pace. Certain parts of your regular runs, such as getting ready to run and cleaning up after a run, take a fixed amount of time. Those two factors don't change whether you run 2 miles or 20. When you become more efficient at running and are therefore doing average runs at a faster pace, the additional time the practice takes is minimized.

Naturally, if you race regularly, increasing your endurance increases your performance at all distances, but especially at the longer distances where endurance is disproportionately rewarded. The extra mileage simply allows your body to go longer better. Also, once you get better at something, you derive more enjoyment from it, which is a motivator to do it better still.

Fortunately, the demographics of the typical runner are spiked with motivation, ambition, and dedication to purpose. Some runners, especially newer arrivals, quite simply don't know how to get better, or they don't realize that they can by making only minor changes to their training regimen.

Here is a good way to add mileage to your training. Set aside a six-month season and experiment with adding a bit of extra mileage each week. Don't add very much. Try adding one extra mile for the first week, two the second week, three the third week, and then drop back the fourth week to your original weekly mileage to give your body a chance to rest. In the second four-week series, add two miles the first week, three the second, four the third, and for the fourth drop back to your original level.

If you started at 30 miles a week, by the sixth month you'll have topped out at 38 miles per week, which doesn't sound like a massive increase, but percentage-wise it is significant. Aside from the 38-mile-per-week peak, it is the extra miles added between 30 and 38 that make you a better, more efficient, and likely faster runner.

Two factors that affect running efficiency are vertical movement and what I call slogging.

Any vertical movement while running requires energy. The higher you move at each step, the more energy you expend. Watch a world-class road racer: you could literally sit a glass of water on his head and it wouldn't spill. This perfection in smooth, efficient forward motion is very apparent when you watch coverage of the New York City Marathon at the 54th Street Bridge. The bridge railing obscures runners' bodies so

that just their heads are visible. Their heads move along the railing as smoothly as bowling balls roll down an alley.

If your head rises 1 inch per stride, and if there are 2,500 strides per mile (measuring each stride at a little more than 2 feet), in a marathon there would be 65,500 strides, and you would have "climbed" 5,458 feet into the air in addition to running 26.2 miles horizontally. How much energy does it take to climb 5,458 feet? It's like climbing a mile-high ladder. If you run more miles to teach your body to run more efficiently, you'll have 5,458 feet of climbing energy to apply to your marathon.

Slogging involves short steps, whereas running involves a longer stride. Consider the increase in performance if you could add 1 inch to each stride. The 65,500 strides in a marathon translates to 65,500 inches, or 5,458 feet (a bit more than a mile), which means that your running self would be finished the marathon while your slogging self would still be more than a mile from the finish line.

In a sport such as long-distance running, inches translate to miles. Fortunately, you do not need to consciously grab at that extra inch per stride. Doing so consciously can cause overstriding problems. The longer stride will come on its own, in part through increased efficiency and in part through being propelled more forcefully through the stride by a more powerful launch, or push-off. In effect, the strength you build up from the additional miles naturally moves you farther along the horizontal plane while minimizing wasted energy on vertical effort caused by bouncing.

Run more miles, allow your body to increase its efficiency and speed, and the rewards can be enormous.

For Your Consideration

- Increased mileage, if applied carefully, increases both performance and form.
- For the average long-distance runner, a little additional mileage has very measurable benefits.
- As long as you add mileage slowly and work easy weeks into your schedule, the additional miles should have no negative effects. In fact, just the opposite should occur.
- Running more miles directly increases your endurance base and therefore your performance in the latter stages of a longer race.
- Racing on a regular basis increases leg speed, and increased leg speed increases the speed and efficiency of your regular weekly training runs.

Comstock

MOVE DOWN
IN MILEAGE

Everyone knows the phrase "Less is more" and knows essentially what it means. The idea is that you will get more out of something by doing it less, assuming that you are doing way too much to start with.

Most long-distance runners today are not doing too much running. This is unlike what was happening during the original running boom of the late-1970s, when even average marathon runners were training 50 to 100 miles a week. Today it is the rare runner who approaches those weekly distances.

Nevertheless, a case can be made that a runner who does less mileage of a higher quality can perform better. Let's take a look at that case by considering the concept of "junk miles" and that of stressing quality over quantity.

The concept of junk miles originated from the army of runners who were putting in megamileage but decided, because of time restraints, to jettison miles that they could not track as contributing significantly to their fitness levels. The concept was very popular with triathletes, especially Ironman-level triathletes, who reigned as the kings (and queens) of time management, always challenged to get in sufficient training at three demanding sports. These upper-tier aerobic athletes were real dynamos in their professional, personal, and sport lives. They didn't have much use for wasted time—in anything. So they sought to trim their sport lives of any effort that was not directly contributing to the desired outcome.

Athletes identified junk miles in a number of ways. If the program called for a hill workout to build strength, and a mile within the workout was not sufficiently steep, it was considered a junk mile and excised from the program. If the lead-in to a track workout usually involved a two-mile warm-up, but the athlete could get away with a one-mile warm-up, one junk mile (and hence roughly eight minutes) was sliced from the athlete's workout.

Some of us have examined the concept of junk miles and have gone somewhat retro, falling back to the 1970s when any mile was a good mile because it added to the total mileage that week. The more total mileage you could get for the week, the more endurance you'd built up.

The other concept that played a major role in the case for reducing mileage was rearranging a training program to stress quality over quantity. Built into this concept was the reality that less had to be more because stressing quality made "more" (i.e., quantity) unattainable because of the risk of overuse injuries. In other words, you could take your current program, which had you on the edge of becoming injured (although it kept you very, very fit; it's a very challenging balancing act), and turn some of the miles into quality miles. In the process, though, you would have to eliminate some miles to give your body a chance

to rest and recuperate. Athletes who could maintain quantity while increasing quality—by keeping mileage but adding more quality to those miles—would certainly improve as athletes, but would likely have to cut back very seriously on the length of time they maintained maximum running performance. In the end, both concepts—eliminating junk miles and stressing quality over quantity—involved fewer weekly miles.

Sometimes lessons like this come about almost by accident. Twice in the 1960s world-record marathon runner Derek Clayton of Australia was sidelined with injuries requiring surgery. Both times he was forced to cut back on his total mileage to a mere maintenance level until he recovered from injuries caused, simply enough, by running too many miles too hard. What was the result? In both cases he came back and broke his own world records. He had, in effect, run himself into injury from too many miles, but by cutting back and relying to some extent on the tremendous base he had built up over the years, he came back better than ever.

Both concepts can be profitably incorporated into the training regimen of even the more casual or time-starved runner today . . . to a point. Eliminating junk miles from your current program or simply not incorporating them into your program to start with seems a simple enough concept, except for the fact that some junk miles are inevitable (such as warm-up or cool-down miles sandwiching more intense workouts) and perhaps even desirable. However, if they are necessary to the success of the training regimen, is it fair to refer to them as junk miles? Probably not.

As an example, if you are scheduled for a Thursday afternoon track workout of four mile repeats with a lap between each, you certainly don't want to go to the track and immediately start with a mile repeat. To do so is to invite (even encourage) injury to cold and stiff muscle tissue. The warm-up miles, then, although not quality miles, are essential miles and certainly not junk. Likewise, you don't want to cut out the one-lap jog between repeat miles, because if you do, you get rid of one junk mile, but you are no longer doing repeat miles; you're doing a four-mile track speed workout.

But any distance run beyond what you actually need *would* qualify as junk miles. For example, using that same Thursday track workout, if the temperature is warm, you might be able to get away with one warm-up mile instead of two because your muscles will already be loosened to some extent by the ambient temperature. Hence, you can get away with losing one junk mile during your warm-up and one during your cool-down after the workout is over.

In the matter of quality versus quantity, excess miles (quantity) could certainly be considered junk miles, but not in all instances. Depending on the distance at which you plan to race, you need a certain base from

which to launch a program, and that base is based on volume, a volume not always steeped in quality miles.

A 50-year-old male who has five years of distance running experience and wants to run a decent marathon four or five months down the road should gradually build to 35 to 45 miles (56 to 72 km) a week for a base. During the base phase, little of that mileage needs to be quality. Quality is typically dialed in later, when hill workouts for strength and speed workouts for increased leg speed and running efficiency are required. At that point, the total volume of mileage can be decreased.

Remember that no matter what distances you want to race at, you need to train like a marathoner, building a wide base. Arthur Lydiard proved that in the 1960s with his New Zealand runners. He believed that a good base of miles was essential to success. He had Peter Snell, an 800-meter specialist, train with the marathoners to build a base. At first Snell hated it, and at one point in the early phase of weekend long runs, he broke down during the middle of the grind and wept. But little by little, he adapted and learned the wisdom of Lydiard's ways when, in the back stretch of the second lap of his Olympic gold medal 800 performance, his legs still felt fresh and full of running.

There is also the matter of learning hard/easy routines, which today are often ignored in favor of either running pretty much the same program each week (with a gradual increase in volume) or running whatever mileage will fit in around everything else going on in life. The value of lower mileage (and less quality) during the easy days or weeks cannot be stressed enough. Once again, you must appreciate the concept that the training effect does not take place while the body is exercising, but rather *after* the exercise happens, as the body repairs itself and recuperates from the workout, becoming stronger and more efficient for the next set of exercises.

The hard/easy training principle is extremely simple and extremely effective, yet when mentioned around many of today's runners, it draws a blank look. It would be valuable to take a few minutes to discuss this very elemental concept and how it (1) increases fitness level and performance and (2) prevents injuries and staleness.

Think of hard/easy as walking up a flight of stairs and taking the elevator down.

We can apply the hard/easy principle to a week's worth of running, a month's worth of running, a year's worth of running, or more. The classic example of more than a year is Finland's Lasse Viren, who peaked for the Olympic Games every fourth year. He took it easy after the Games, then gradually built over the next three years toward the next Olympics.

On a weekly basis, the hard/easy principle incorporates easy days after hard days; hard days would be the weekend long run or the weekly

track speed workout. On a four-week basis, hard/easy would apply this way: Week 1 would be medium hard. Week 2 would be a bit harder than week 1. Week 3 would be harder than week 2. And week 4 would involve cutting back on the severity of the training to give the body some rest and some time for recuperation before going hard again. The key week here is week 4, the easy week.

The best workout in the world doesn't contribute anything positive unless it is allowed to ferment within the cask of rest, which is where the training effect really takes place. Sometimes cutting back total weekly mileage can contribute to better and safer running. You should consider this especially when planning downtimes during the yearly seasonal calendar. (See chapter 16 on rest.)

For Your Consideration

- When in doubt, do less.
- The training effect takes place during the recuperation from a hard workout.
- Learn the hard/easy concept, and apply it to your training year-round.
- Unless you are an elite athlete, never do back-to-back quality workouts.
- Consider the possibility that junk miles do not exist.

Imago/Icon SMI

CREATE ADVENTURE RUNS

with

Dean Karnazes

People who are critical of long-distance running often cite the fact that they see very few people smile as they run. It looks to outsiders as though running is painful and boring. The response of the runner, of course, is that once you get past the first two months, it is no longer boring. It is, in fact, invigorating and refreshing—whether it looks that way from the outside or not.

In actuality, for some runners, running *can* get boring. It all depends on the runner's personality. I know a woman who year after year ran the same 10-mile course five or six days a week. To her, repeatedly running the same course wasn't boring. To some of us, however, it might very well go in that direction.

To keep running from becoming boring, some people schedule at least one annual special run, often on a birthday. Some runners run the number of years old they are on that special day. Of course, once you get past a certain age, you're well into eating up most of your birthday by ultrarunning. But there's nothing wrong with that. Some runners invite their friends to come out to run some of the birthday miles with them and turn the event into a mobile party, capped off with a traditional birthday party afterward.

One tried-and-true way to add excitement to your running is to schedule an adventure run at least once a year. What's an adventure run? It's a specially tailored run in which you go somewhere significant or symbolic. You essentially depart on a road trip—but without the car. Think of Jack Kerouac's Dean Moriarty and Sal Paradise from his novel *On the Road* doing it all with shoe leather rather than tire rubber.

Some runners cross their home states in adventure runs. In July of 1989 my friend Tom Crawford and I put together an adventure run from Badwater in Death Valley to the peak of Mt. Whitney and back. We referred to it as an adventure run because if we thought of it in terms of a huge physical challenge, we probably would have found we were not up to it. By referring to it as an adventure run, we could minimize the danger and challenge and think of it more in terms of going somewhere on foot.

Runners have fashioned adventure runs into transcontinental jaunts from Los Angeles to New York or from the West Coast of Sonoma County in Northern California to Hilton Head, South Carolina, as the elderly Paul Reese did. Dave McGillivray, the race director of the Boston Marathon, once ran from Medford, Oregon, to Medford, Massachusetts. There have even been runners who have attempted to run around the world—and at least one we know of who succeeded.

You don't need to go to that extreme, certainly, but scheduling an annual adventure run has a certain charm and provides a pivotal point to your year's worth of running. For those who are also fond of

planning and organizing trips, vacations, and their lives in general, an adventure run is a huge bonus. And the more of your friends you can get involved in the process, the better. Turn it into a big annual party.

I'm personally not fond of birthday bashes in which runners go to a track for the day and run the number of miles that correspond to their age, because running around a track doesn't fit my concept of an adventure run. Although it is symbolic on many levels and is easy to organize, *it doesn't go anywhere*. Where's the adventure if all you see all day is the same thing?

I'm much more fond of the extremely creative adventure runs put together by folks such as Utah's Davy Crockett. (Yes, his name is actually Davy Crockett!) Ole Davy's deal is that, section by section, he is running the Pony Express Trail through the state of Utah. Because the trail has not been kept up well through most of the state, and because some folks have built housing developments over some of it, to run the trail accurately, Davy has to do a lot of research in advance of his runs. The research is half the fun because, as he reads up on various sections of the trail, Davy becomes an authority on the history of various way stations, specific Pony Express riders, and towns that were either built up along the trail or turned into ghost towns as soon as the trail was closed.

Kenneth Williams from Corinth, Mississippi, put together a run across the state of Mississippi that he fashioned as a fund-raiser for Boys' and Girls' Clubs of Mississippi. Along the way he stopped off at schools and gave talks about the importance of fitness for people of all ages. In all, he spoke to more than 10,000 kids.

Your adventure run doesn't have to be quite so grandiose—at least not the first year you fashion one. Start small, and see how it goes. Then, if you enjoy it, you can build on it in future years. You have the option of going off quietly and doing an adventure run on your own or going to the other extreme and turning it into a big show to which you invite all your friends to do some or all of it with you.

There are numerous rails-to-trails paths throughout the country—running, walking, and biking paths built on the abandoned rail beds of defunct railroads. You could research the defunct railroad that once owned the line and put together a run that follows the trail from one end to the other. Runners living in the Washington, D.C., area can run the old C&O Canal path.

Several runners have taken a couple of months and run the Appalachian Trail from Georgia to Maine. Others have run the John Muir Trail along the backbone of the Sierra Nevada in California. Still others have run the length of historic Route 66 from Santa Monica in Southern California to Chicago.

An adventure run can take anywhere from an afternoon to several months. The crux of it is to pick something that is challenging but that you know you can do if you build toward it and plan it out well. In the process, go somewhere, travel by foot from point A to point B. Then celebrate, and immediately start planning next year's adventure run.

This is an excellent way of energizing your running as well as sharing it with family and friends.

Although the concept of the adventure run has come into its own in recent years, it is not entirely new. In fact, it is more of a revival than a fresh trend. The height of popularity of the adventure trek by foot was the period from the mid-1800s to the end of that century when the pedestrian movement flourished, as mentioned in chapter 10. Hardy adventurers such as Edward Payson Weston put together tremendous treks that pitted them against themselves, against others, and against the clock. Weston began his career with a challenge he accepted to travel on foot to Lincoln's inauguration in the winter of 1861. He left the State House in Boston on February 22 and reached Washington, D.C., on March 4 (453 miles, or 729 kilometers, in 208 hours), missing his goal by half a day because of horrendous weather and road conditions. The pedestrian, go-as-you-please contests became professional affairs and were enormously popular, but they eventually wore themselves out because of overexposure and were replaced by multi-day bicycle races.

Transcontinental treks were revived in the 1960s (from the ashes of the Bunion Derbies in 1928 and 1929) and were usually solo affairs with limited or no support. (See Jim Shapiro's *Meditations From the Breakdown Lane* in the online appendix B, 25 Running Books You Should Read, http://tinyurl.com/35g17mg.)

Similarly, adventure runs put together in the 1960s traversed challenging terrain. A course was created from Shoshone in southern Death Valley to Scotty's Castle in the north. The course was later altered to run from Badwater to Mt. Whitney.

Adventure runs have been escalating in popularity again over the past two decades both to provide bragging rights and to serve as a new and unique approach to keeping runners always reaching beyond the next horizon. Certainly, whatever adventure run the mind can conceive, the runner—with proper preparation—can do. And let's face it, there is no more intimate way to see the sights along the way than to travel on foot.

My favorite adventure runner is Dean Karnazes, the author of *Ultramarathon Man: Confessions of an All-Night Runner* and an outstanding endurance runner. He once ran 50 marathons in 50 states in 50 days. He ran the string of all 22 missions in California that sit between Sonoma

and San Diego. He also ran more than 300 miles without sleeping. He often runs the 100 miles from his home in the Bay Area to the start of the Napa Valley Marathon, runs the race, and then runs home. His whole life is an adventure run. He told me about his idea of a manageable adventure run any decent runner can construct. He calls it a runabout:

The legendary running coach Jeff Galloway has probably trained more marathoners than anyone on earth. Jeff teaches a unique training system that includes regular, brief walking periods. He's also among the few running coaches who encourage those athletes preparing for a marathon to do training runs exceeding 26.2 miles (including the walking segments). Those who follow this advice report that the inclusion of walking segments makes these "overdistance" workouts perfectly manageable. Going beyond the distance of the actual race is also a great confidence builder, especially for first-timers.

I recommend a slight modification to Jeff's approach that I simply call Runabout. Inspired by the Australian Aboriginal practice of Walkabout, it works like this: After you've put in some good training and built a fairly decent level of fitness, pick a weekend morning to set out from the front door of your house with a running pack, the contents of which should include some cash, a credit card, a cell phone, some fluid, and some snacks—maybe also a map or a GPS if you want to get really sophisticated. Choose a direction (e.g., north) and start running. Keep running until you feel like taking a break, but don't. Just slow down and jog or walk, but don't stop moving. The important thing is to keep upright and maintain forward progress. If you get really tired, run by Starbucks and grab a latte. Stick a straw in it and drink it as you shuffle along.

Try to make a complete day of the outing. Better, end up at one of your favorite nearby resorts or spas, and make an evening of it as well. Don't worry about how many miles you actually run. Focus instead on keeping on your feet and on moving forward, one way or another (be it running, jogging, hiking, or walking), for at least six to eight hours. Mostly, have fun and enjoy the experience.

Not only will you get a great workout, but also it's an interesting and spontaneous way to spend a day (or series of days). Funny things happen out there. You have chance encounters, you see things you wouldn't normally see during your typical daily runs, and it can be quite captivating. Rarely in our modern society do we spend an entire day outside, and there's just something enchanting and magical about watching a day go by from the exterior of a building rather than being stuck inside one. There's a lot to be learned from those Aboriginals, despite not having a single Starbucks in the Outback.

For Your Consideration

- Consider making an annual adventure run the culmination of your running year.

- Plan an adventure run that ties in another interest, whether it be a fascination with national parks, defunct railroads, or famous roadways.

- Get your family and friends involved, both in the planning and in the execution of the adventure run itself. It's always more fun to share these sorts of crazy adventures than it is to do them solo.

- Be as creative as you can with organizing your adventure run, even going so far as to have special celebratory T-shirts made up for the occasion.

- Commission one of your friends who is good with a video camera to film the whole affair, and then edit the adventure down to an hour documentary that you can share with friends and that constitutes a permanent record of your accomplishment.

Susan Rae Tannenbaum/fotolia.com

RUN UNDER CONTROL

For many a runner—especially a long-distance runner—learning to run "under control" (that is, with self-control and discipline) is more difficult than training to race in the first place. How many runners have you heard use the phrase "I run without a plan"?

How often does running like you feel get you where you want to be as far as a time goal in the marathon goes? The marathon is a race designed for the patient, disciplined, under control personality.

Various lures and obstacles embedded in the marathon can guarantee that if you run without a plan, you will court disaster every time you line up at a starting line.

Let's consider just a few:

• The tapering period (the two to three weeks leading to the marathon itself) brings together the strength and endurance of 16 to 18 weeks of hard training, so that you arrive at the starting line filled with enormous reserves of energy: both physical and nervous. Unless you are heavily disciplined, you will allow the built-up energy to dictate the early pace, which leads to disaster because you cover the first half of the race way too fast and have little left for the bitter final miles.

• You have practiced discipline in the early miles because you have (finally) had enough disasters on the road from going out too fast at the starting gun to have gotten the point. But then you hit the extremely sweet midportion of the race, between 7 and 16 miles, when the deepest parts of your big leg muscles are warmed and supple and your stride is smooth and rhythmic. You are in such a heaven of wonderful running that you conclude that in some magical way the training has gone better than expected and you are in much better shape than anticipated, so hey, let's go for it! You allow your legs to run as fluidly and as smoothly and as fast as ever they want, and what happens? Not only do they use up the energy reserved for that portion of the race, but they also leech some of the energy that's being saved for the final miles. By the time you, the incredibly powerful runner, reach 22 miles, you are no longer so powerful or smooth or filled with running, and the final miles become a nightmare.

• An important embedded obstacle to consider is failure to monitor. You need to constantly monitor what your body is doing throughout the race: your breathing, your heart rate, the striking of your feet on the asphalt pavement, your arm swing, the position of your hips, and your perspiration rate. Like an airline pilot, and the conscientious and patient marathoner that you are, you monitor all systems. You do not "run wild" or "run as you feel like it" simply because during the early portions of the race, if you've done the training, you're going to feel mighty wonderful. But that seeming invincibility never lasts.

What are the best ways to make sure you don't fall victim to these three potential problems?

1. Going into the taper phase, carefully write down what workouts you should be doing each day—and at what effort level. Review the list each day of the taper, and stick to it. When you line up on race day, have your race carefully calculated. Race pace wristbands are readily available. Don't ever assume that the fact that you are in a race will magically bring your per-mile pace down. Line up in the field approximately where you think you'll end up at the finish. If you are doing a nine-minute mile, don't line up in the front row: you'll be in the way of faster runners, and you'll be tempted to go out too fast when everyone around you goes out in a rush. Because of the excellent condition you are in, the first miles will seem painfully easy. Restrain yourself. Putting money or time in the bank in the early miles by running faster than planned doesn't pay off in the final miles.

2. In those wonderfully invigorating middle miles of a marathon, discipline is of prime importance. Consult your race pace wristband and stick to your pre-race calculations. Enjoy the experience of strong, efficient running. The more disciplined you can be in those miles, the longer the euphoric feeling will last, possibly taking you blissfully into the 20-mile mark, and perhaps beyond.

3. Think of yourself as a race car. Run through a checklist of body systems to monitor at each mile. Because thinking straight in the last miles of a marathon becomes more and more difficult, write a list on your wrist or upside down on the underside of your race number: *breathing, arm carriage, leg rhythm, head carriage, perspiration,* and so on.

Keep in mind that much of what applies to a marathon applies also to shorter races. When I lived in the Napa Valley, I used to do a lot of 10K road races. I became friends with one fellow who consistently, every race, went out too fast, and I consistently passed him around mile 4 of every 10K we ran. After the races, I'd ask him why he didn't pace himself better. "That's just how I race," he explained, which kind of explained nothing. Whether the race is a 5K or a marathon, know your projected pace per mile going into the race, settle into that pace, and stick to it. Try to run an even-paced race. It's easier on your body and it is sure satisfying to the mind to know that when you cross the finish line, you'll have metered out your best throughout the race.

The matter of running under control extends to two other areas of concern: basic training and the frequency of racing, both of which relate

directly to satisfaction—or lack thereof—in the runner's realm of racing. Many runners these days cheat themselves out of a full and fulfilling running or racing experience by not preparing properly for race day and by not carefully laying out the training period leading up to the race. Their training sessions are either haphazard or halfhearted, not well thought out or executed in a less-than-maximum method.

Some runners don't even bother to lay out a training program. Instead, they run when they find the time or feel the inclination. Then they are personally disappointed in the results of their racing. Running races are one of the only arenas in life in which great expectations are anticipated based on weak investments. (The others are the stock market and the state lottery.)

A term paper at school, an end-of-quarter report at work, building a house, even washing a car are all accomplished in a logical, methodical manner. If certain steps are not followed, or if a few steps are skipped, the project falls apart and is a disaster. The same is true of a training program toward running a race. To do well in the race takes planning and dedication in the preparation. You get out of a race what you put into the training leading up to it.

What makes the long-distance racing scene so fascinating is that it isn't a game of checkers; it's a game of chess. Key workouts must be sandwiched between "filler" workouts in which you run easy to recover; the hard/easy method must be closely adhered to, to avoid injury and burnout. On race day you must go into the race fully cognizant of your current ability; and in the race itself, you must use extreme discipline to have enough energy and speed left in the final mile to squeeze out that extra second or two.

To do well in racing, you've got to dedicate a certain amount of time and energy to the process leading up to it. The race itself is the cherry on top of the sundae. To regard the rest of it as a chore is to lose yourself outside the process. In disciplined running, the process is all.

As I've said many times, the sport of long-distance running and racing has accumulated a great storehouse of knowledge over many centuries and many billions of miles run. Numerous knowledgeable and practical books and Web sites are available with well-proven training programs for virtually every distance imaginable. If it comes to a choice between a Web site and a book, always choose the book. Why? Because numerous trained professionals have had an opportunity to review, closely, every line in the book, whereas any yahoo can throw up a Web site.

If you insist on using a Web site, make sure it is being managed by someone whose name you recognize for his or her long history of teaching runners to run well: Joe Henderson, Lorraine Moller, Hal Higdon, Jeff Galloway, Mike Schreiber, or Gordon Bakoulis. And stick faithfully

to the program. Sure, you can still do well in a race after skipping a few of the marginal workouts; but skip one of the critical workouts (such as the weekend long run), and you're asking for yet another disastrous race experience.

Running under control involves sticking to a plan, whether in a daily workout or in a race. Sticking to a plan is important in daily workouts because it is one piece in a greater puzzle. If you deviate from the established plan, you chance mangling the day's puzzle piece.

Easy days are dialed in for a very good reason: they are there to massage the muscles of the legs after a hard workout from the previous day, and to keep the legs in the habit of running. It is not uncommon for a runner to run too fast or hard on an easy day. To see how important it is to go slow, watch some of the masterful Kenyans when they go out for a workout. They speed up once they are deep into the workout, but when they start, they shuffle along as though they were just learning to jog. They know the importance of very gradually warming up the leg muscles.

Additionally, learning to run under control during workouts is excellent practice for race day. Racing under control means entering races fresh, not attempting to race every weekend either because you're trying to create a reputation for yourself as a megaracer or because you are obsessed with running and racing. Obsessions lead only to burnout and frustration, and are an admission that something other than you is in control of your actions. If you are obsessed, you have deeded control of yourself to what amounts to a compulsion. Moreover, logic and reason have been stomped into the mud and are no longer available as tools to improve or control your training and racing.

Let's look at the race experience. A race, by definition, is a contest that pits you over the distance against the clock, against yourself, and against others. Someone who is truly racing can perform well only a limited number of times per year. The shorter the race, the more times the distance can be contested. World-class marathoners will tell you that they can pull off only two top-performance marathons per year, usually one in the spring and one in the fall.

But even races at shorter distances demand payment from your body and your head. And they demand down time for recovery. The typical formula is one day of easy running for every mile raced.

Runners who jog through races can literally jog a race every weekend, but they are accomplishing nothing more than logging miles. Ten years down the road, with hundreds of pedestrian 10Ks and dozens of mediocre marathons on their resumes, if they were honest (and, later in their careers, some of them are), most of the jogging racers would gladly trade 100 lame 10Ks for one sub-40:00.

Run under control, follow a sensible and proven program, and the 40-minute 10Ks, the sub-three-hour marathons, and the under-10-hour 50-milers become a possibility.

There are, of course, exceptions, the outliers, the physiological freaks. We know one fellow from Maine who is closing in on his 50th sub-three-hour marathon. Nice accomplishment, but it pales in comparison to Michigan runner Doug Kurtis, who in his career ran 76 sub-2:20 marathons! But guess what? The fellow from Maine and Doug both monitored the reactions of their bodies to training and racing, and they applied that hard-won knowledge to learn how to train and race very much under control.

Observers of the scene continue to weave fantasies about runners who run as they feel like it or who run wild. For decades people pointed at Rhode Island Narragansett Indian runner Ellison "Tarzan" Brown, who reputedly trained little and ran how he felt like. We now know, thanks to Michael Ward's extensive biography, that before the 1936 Boston Marathon (which he won convincingly), he and his coach went off to a quiet cabin in the woods and trained scientifically and extensively. During the actual race, Tarzan did not go out at a sprint to lead and dominate the entire race. He laid back, conserved his resources, and when the time was right, made his move.

You don't even need to race to gain a great deal by running under control. Runners who never race benefit greatly—both in running longevity and in injury avoidance—by mentally running through their upcoming workout in advance, by visualizing the workout before it happens. If you are a long-term runner (but not a racer), you know pretty well what a 10-mile workout at a nine-minute-per-mile pace feels like. And you know what will happen if that is your plan and you go out either too fast or too slow. Too fast, and the final miles will be hell. Too slow, and you'll never get into that comfortable rhythm that makes a well-run long workout so satisfying.

There are certainly some classic examples in world-class racing of finding that comfortable rhythm. Three examples in the Olympic marathon come to mind: Frank Shorter at Munich in 1972, Joan Benoit-Samuelson at Los Angeles in 1984, and Constantina Tomescu-Dita at Beijing in 2008. In all three instances, the runners had trained long and well and were at their peak on race day. Unfortunately for the rest of the field, the early leaders decided to set a pedestrian pace in the hope of forcing a strategic race. But at such a slow pace, Shorter, Benoit-Samuelson, and Tomescu-Dita couldn't find their rhythms, couldn't get comfortable, because it wasn't the pace they'd trained for. So, in essence, they said, "Screw this!" and picked up the pace until they hit the stride they'd been training for. In all three cases, the rest

of the pack decided to let them go, assuming that they'd falter and drift back, to be reabsorbed by the pack.

If you ever have a chance to watch a video of the 1984 women's Olympic marathon, there is one quick scene on the deserted freeway in which Benoit-Samuelson looks behind her to see where her pursuers are—and they aren't there. You have to watch carefully to catch it, but Joan turns back around with such a look of scorn and disdain on her face that it is almost startling.

Naturally, all three went on to win. They never did falter and drift back to be reabsorbed by the pack. And there was no way, on that day, that the pack could pull it together to catch them.

To do well in long-distance (and in life) requires patience, a willingness to delay gratification, self-control, and certainly a sense of pacing—your pacing. Run wild at your own peril. But learn to run under control, and the lessons can be transferred to any number of aspects of your life.

For Your Consideration

- Control and discipline do not a prison make. Some parents want to let their kids go unrestrained through life so as not to curb their creativity, not realizing that before you can draw outside the lines, you need to learn to draw inside the lines. Check out Picasso's early figure drawings.

- A carefully drawn training program is a thing of beauty—and a road map to success.

- Run under control during a race, and the race is yours; run how you feel like, and the race owns you.

- If you have a choice of consulting the Web or a book for training advice, go for the paper solution.

- If you run as you feel like during a race, you are guaranteed of some grim final miles.

Photodisc/Getty Images

RUN WILD

with

Lorraine Moller

Young children, those little sacks of raw energy, left to their own devices, resemble wild animals in their enthusiasm for life and movement. Watch a litter of puppies or kittens, and their every waking moment consists of roughhousing—everything from gnawing on mom's ear, to wrestling with a sibling, to running around in circles for no discernable purpose. Toss a half-dozen little kids into a room and walk away and their antics are similar. They run around randomly, cavort, jump up and down in the same spot, wrestle with each other, and squeal with the joy of just plain living, existing, moving.

Certainly we need to control, to some extent, acts of randomness. Society needs rules and limits or it faces ruin from anarchy and insanity.

In every sort of formal sporting arena, the most that can be accomplished comes in the wake of serious and methodical practice. The young gymnast practices the dismount from the parallel bars over and over and over, until it becomes second nature. The swimming competitor logs endless hours in the pool developing endurance and form that would make a dolphin jealous. The runner builds endurance and strength and speed in the hope of bringing them all together on the day of an important race. For an event such as the marathon, that process may encompass 16 or 18 weeks of carefully laid-out combinations of long runs, tempo runs, speed work at the track, easy runs for muscle recovery, carefully scheduled rest days, and often training in other sports in the hope of continuing to build endurance while preventing injuries.

If you want to succeed, careful training to a plan is not an option. It is everything. And for the obsessive runner, it is anything but a chore. The process of filling in the blanks in a training journal as the workouts progress brings incredible satisfaction. Certainly, training too hard for too long can become mind numbing and burdensome, and often ruinous to one's physical health. But such training does not go on at the same level year-round. If it did, the running body would soon become the broken body.

There are usually two off-seasons: the heart of summer (when it is too hot to run too much) and the depths of winter (when it is too foul outside to do more than maintenance running). These periods provide a welcome relief from the regimen of regular training. And the annual inception of those off-seasons provides an opportunity to be a child again, to live like an animal, to burn off excess fitness, to run wild, and to make the transition from one training period to the next.

Think of your off-season as burning the rice paddies. By that I mean getting rid of the period of training you just left just as rice farmers, once the crop is harvested and the remaining stubble has died and dried out, burn the chaff so that, after a period of rest, the planting and growing process can begin again. This burning of the rice paddies

can be a glorious period twice a year when the excess training you have accumulated so carefully can be burned off in runs that are too fast, too long, or too meandering to be part of any sane running program.

The end of your season is a time to finally run wild. There are no dire consequences to your racing program if you do because your racing program, for this portion of the year, is behind you.

The end of the fall marathon season was always a wonderful time for me to get into the woods and do a long, fartlek-style cross-country run, being careful, at least when I lived back in Pennsylvania or was visiting home, to wear red while romping through the woods because the period corresponded with hunting season. It is a glorious time on the razor's edge, between the end of autumn and the coming of winter, when the air is chilly, the leaves have fallen, the sky is leaden, and you run into a cloud of your own expelled breath. I would do these runs when my legs were a bit tired from the just-passed racing season, but they still had a little spring left that I wanted to leave on the trail before the snows came.

Some runners burn off whatever training effect they have left from the autumn and then go into a whole month of absolutely no running, giving their legs a chance to heal before resuming easy, longer training in preparation for the spring season. The same process can be incorporated into the late spring when the season is ending and you are headed toward maintenance running through the hot, humid summer months. One last hard, long, sweaty, wild run to cap off the racing season is a terrific way to close down shop, burning off the fumes of the just-passed season, and changing gears toward going easy before beginning to rebuild. As long as you don't run yourself into injury on that season-ending hard run, you can consider it a freeing of the animal side of your running, while putting an exclamation mark at the end of the season.

An open period is a perfect opportunity to run wild to build strength, endurance, and flexibility, especially if you have been doing your training exclusively on roads. Take a day to run wild on the trails. This serves several purposes: It breaks up your regular training and thereby freshens it; it provides an opportunity to build strength by running up and down hills; it increases flexibility in the legs and ankles by running over changing terrain (something you don't get running on pavement); it requires some eye–leg coordination to anticipate leaping over roots and rocks; and as far as effort goes, it is like doing a fartlek or track workout when you chug up the hills and coast down the other side.

Wild woodland runs like this can be done to near-exhaustion to great effect if you are willing to really dial back the workouts for the several days following, so that you can properly recuperate. Because of the trail

surface, your legs probably will not take the beating they usually do on asphalt, and your legs and ankles will go through a tremendous range of motion, which they usually don't get to do on pavement.

When we lived in Palo Alto, California, we often ran in Foothills Park. The longest trail in the park essentially did a loop around the perimeter; it was six miles long, with plenty of ups and downs. One year, while training for a fall marathon, instead of doing my scheduled 18-miler on the roads, I decided to run wild and attempt to do the Los Trancos Trail three times. I would have at least two aid stations as I came by the parking lot after the first and second loops, I'd get plenty of strength built up in my legs, I would certainly increase my endurance, and I'd get some leg speed on the well-groomed long downhill trails on the front side of the trail. (The backside was more crude and unkempt, and mostly uphill.)

The other enticing thing about running this trail was that, as far we knew, nobody had ever done it three times. So it would be a wild ride, indeed. And it turned out to be just that. In the middle of the third lap, a storm complete with a low-rolling, chilling fog came in, and the temperature dropped a good 20 °F (11 °C). Although tired, I had to keep moving at a decent clip just to keep my muscles warm. It remains one of the most memorable runs I've ever done over the last 40 years.

Almost as memorable, but for a vastly different reason, was a run a bit farther south, in the hills above Los Altos. Amby Burfoot, then the East Coast editor of *Runner's World*, was in town for some editorial meetings. He wanted to do a trail run. Sounded good to me. Unfortunately, some of the meetings we were attending went late (as usual). We ran from publisher Bob Anderson's house in Los Altos Hills, heading up one of the trailheads at twilight. Then we proceeded to get lost. Then it began to get dark. We could see the lights of houses far below us, but every time we took a different trail, it ended in a wall of greenery we couldn't penetrate or a barbed-wire fence.

Eventually, we came out in someone's backyard, managed to avoid a confrontation with the owner's dog, and jumped out onto the paved road, where we jogged back to Bob's house. Once there, we (dumbly, as it turned out) jumped into the hot tub. What that served to do was heat up and further distribute the oil of the poison oak bushes we'd run through, so that later that night Amby and I looked like zombies as we lathered ourselves with calamine lotion. We still talk about running wild in those hills above Los Altos, and as far as I know, neither of us has broken our pact to never again run in strange woods after dark.

I remember a runner who lived and ran (a lot) in the Great Southwest. His name is John Annerino, and he made a reputation for himself as the guy who ran wild in the southwestern deserts. He even wrote a book

about it: *Running Wild: An Extraordinary Adventure of the Human Spirit* (1992, 1998, Thunder's Mouth Press). In one of his crazy runs, he ran 750 miles from Mexico to Utah. The *LA Times* reviewed the book this way: "He nearly drowned. He battled heat, cold, thirst and exhaustion. When he was nearly done, a snake rattled inches away from his ankles." Now that's memorable running.

In running wild, there is also a great cleansing involved that crosses all cultures and that plumbs the depths of the human spirit. Cleansing by excess perspiration is seen in many cultures as a sacred ritual.

Of course, too much running wild can have a damning effect. "The most horrific runner in literature of the nineteenth or any century," Roger Robinson wrote in his 2003 book *Running in Literature*, "must be the Polynesian cannibal priest, dressed only in the hair of the dead, who in a little-known Robert Louis Stevenson ballad runs in a frenzied nonstop three-day ritual before naming the victims for the next feast" (p. 127). The final line of the poem reads: "The wreck of the red-eyed priest came gasping home in the dusk." Obviously, too much of a good thing.

Call it what you will—running wild, burning the rice paddies, running as you feel—it can be one of the most memorable and meaningful runs of your entire year—the very antithesis of running under control.

I asked Lorraine Moller how she would characterize that letting-it-loose run at the end of the season. Lorraine was born and raised in New Zealand where, as a youngster, she and her friends typically ran without shoes and frequently ran wild through the woods, something she still remembers fondly. Lorraine was one of the dominant female road runners in the 1980s, especially in the marathon. She won three of the Avon International Women's Marathons; nobody else won more than one. She won the Boston Marathon in 1984 and the Osaka Ladies' Marathon three times. She competed in the first four women's Olympic marathons, winning the bronze in 1992.

In a typical Lorraine way, her response to my question came back in the form of a poem:

> *Second Wind*
>
> *I run.*
> *I run away from*
> *Gravity of wrongs lived and relived*
> *The sword that silences my song*
> *The trance that eats my life.*
> *Survival of the swift*
> *It is written in salt.*
> *I run.*
> *I run towards*

The distant mother of the familiar unknown
Great Big Simplicity.
AHA!
I see new realms in your footprints
Wild One.
In-between away and towards
There is the place of the Second Wind
The still place between breaths.
Anyone unhurried can find it
Even the timid.
Shh, not a word
Run with me
And I will meet you there.

Obviously, Lorraine has on occasion run wild, as anyone who knows her will readily confirm. For the obsessive/compulsive long-distance runner, an occasional wild run could provide all sorts of benefits, especially liberation from the usual and mundane.

For Your Consideration

- Follow the dictates of nature: schedule rest periods at the beginning of summer and the beginning of winter. And celebrate these with a wild run or two.

- Define a logical racing season—and then stick with it, even if your racing is going unusually well. To overdo it is to invite injury. After your scheduled season, celebrate with an unstructured romp. (If you are worried about doing something so out of the ordinary for you, put your cell phone in your fanny pack, just in case.)

- Once the racing season ends, you are no longer restrained by the niceties of structure and regimen, so take an unscheduled run or two based on simple abandon.

- Run over hill and dale until you run yourself out; then cut your training back radically and allow your minute muscle tears and injuries to heal before restarting your training for another season of racing.

REST

with

Marshall Ulrich

Every time you turn around, there are reports of how overworked and overtired Americans are. A recent study concluded that Americans have no more leisure time today than they had in 1900 (*Harper's Magazine,* June 2007, p. 13). I think back to the 1950s when, inspired by the space race, scientists and sociologists were spending an inordinate amount of time gazing raptly into the ideal future overflowing with outrageous laborsaving devices.

As it turned out, nothing much came of all the daydreaming of futures filled with fun and leisure. If you want leisure time, you've gotta live in Europe, where they get five weeks off at a time (usually the same five weeks in the middle of summer) and all go to the same beaches to relax like fleas on a poodle.

For most Americans, on the other hand, a 40-hour workweek just doesn't get it done. And if you're a salaried employee or self-employed, you get to work just as many hours as you can stand. It's no wonder there are dozens of sleep-aid ads in magazines and on television. It's no wonder people are turning their cars into mobile offices.

The experts contend that, when you finally do drag yourself to bed, if it takes less than three minutes to fall asleep, you are overtired. (Of course, you don't want the opposite problem, either: insomnia that causes you to never get to sleep, sometimes caused by walking around all day in a semislumber.)

Marching through life in an overtired state isn't good for a person's health, and it certainly isn't good for a person's equanimity. This may be why so many people try to construct an even keel by enrolling in everything from aromatherapy to yoga to book discussion clubs to quilting bees. (No joke. The latter is making a comeback as a way of relaxing, helping the local community, and socializing with a group of like-minded folks.)

The surrender to a continuous feeling of tiredness splashes over into long-distance running. People who are very serious about their running are frequently not serious enough about the resting phase of their training. And it's the resting phase of a training program where the training effect actually takes place. Dave Costill, the godfather of human performance studies, put it very simply in his book *Running: The Athlete Within*: "Balance work and rest. The purpose of training is to stimulate the runner's anatomy and physiology to grow stronger during periods of rest and repair. Without adequate rest, the benefits of training cannot be fully realized (p. 103)."

You can train yourself into the ground, but if you don't back off and give your body (and mind and spirit) time to recover from the workouts, the training effect never has a chance to kick in, and the workouts are nothing more than self-flagellation.

Consider the fact that any training you do is a process of breaking down your muscles. Run a hard 10-mile workout and your muscles are stressed and strained and, to an extent, damaged. You can't do too many hard workouts too frequently without inviting injury or breakdown. A running journal can be educational when you suffer an overuse injury, because you can then put on your deer slayer cap and clench that pipe firmly in the side of your mouth and get out that magnifying glass; then, in the guise of Sherlock Holmes, you can peruse the last two or three weeks of your training journal and determine just where you started to hurt yourself.

As we've already discussed, overuse injuries don't happen overnight. It's traumatic injuries that occur suddenly, like when you trip on the curb of the sidewalk and fall down. Overuse injuries, as we've discussed before, are like the mist on the windshield of a car. When enough mist falls, the droplets begin to run one into another, in the process forming ever-larger drops that slide down the windshield, encounter other drops, clot together and make still bigger drops. That's how an overuse injury happens: little tears joining other little tears to finally come together to make big tears—and big tears are overuse injuries.

If you stop the misting process, eventually the droplets evaporate and you're no worse for the wear you've laid on your muscles. The way to stop the misting process is to rest.

Rest doesn't have to be total inactivity that makes you feel as though you've encased yourself in a complete body cast. Gentle physical activity (taking a stroll, puttering in the garden, or walking the dog) can be a form of active rest. The object is to stay away from more running for a period of time so that your body can undergo the training effect. The result is that when your next scheduled workout comes along, your muscles are at an increased level of fitness and ready for an additional workload.

This need for rest is why most professional runners don't have regular jobs. Part of their job is taking a quality nap in the afternoon between the morning and the late-afternoon workout. They also get regular massages to expedite the recovery process from their training, which is both high quality and high quantity. They also need to psychologically rest so they can recuperate from recent races and more demanding strength training workouts, such as hill work.

For most of us who are stitching our training in around the quiltwork of real life, getting in the necessary rest periods can be difficult. But if we are to perform well in races and if we are to continue training without incurring injury, we definitely need to accommodate the body's need for restorative rest.

Of course, there is also a flip side these days. Some runners expect to run well on more rest than training. Runners who train little but expect

decent results have spent too much time in the modern school system where everyone who shows up gets a gold star. Or, if you show up late but not quite as late as last week, you are also praised and rewarded. Or, if you merely exist, you expect praise.

Long-distance running rewards hard work. There are no shortcuts, no matter how many claims you hear that this or that food will knock five minutes off your next 10K. The rewards of long-distance running are earned the hard way: one step at a time. The successful long-distance runner is a master of pacing, hard work, and appropriate rest.

You don't need to run 120 miles a week to get a decent marathon time—especially if you are already working full-time or beyond.

You can run a marathon you can be proud of on 55 to 75 miles (89 to 121 km) a week. The 120-mile-per-week (193 km) load is for the national- and international-class runners. But you won't run a decent marathon on 25 to 35 (40 to 56 km) miles a week—unless you've been at it a long time and your legs have a lot of muscle memory miles on them. Memory miles come from those long, hard weeks of training over a decade or more that hard-wires your legs to know what is required of them when you pin on a number. But that seemingly magical phenomenon can be tapped only so many times.

For the good runner, hard work is a must. As is hard rest, which could include a well-placed nap. Naps are silver bullets against exhaustion.

Although it is impractical to take a nap during a fiercely fought 10K or even in a marathon, it is not unusual for ultrarunners to take naps during hundred-milers, especially during the dark hours. I know a woman who ran the Western States 100 and, midway through the night portion, just could not go on. She was exhausted. Her pacer advised her to lie down beside the trail and take a half-hour nap. Ten minutes later the pacer woke her up and she was filled with energy and raring to go. "I feel great," she responded. "That was the best half-hour I ever spent sleeping." Of course, the pacer never told her she'd been down for a mere 10 minutes.

As members of a society built on guilt, and as people on whom guilt is often heaped (sometimes even by ourselves), it is sometimes difficult to feel comfortable taking that well-earned, strategic rest period without feeling guilty—and nothing interrupts a perfectly good nap more effectively than a rash of guilt for taking the nap (or from questioning whether you are napping correctly).

If you train hard, race often, but pace yourself wisely, give yourself a break. The following guidelines can help you determine whether you are failing to get enough rest:

- You fall asleep in the evening within three minutes of your head hitting the pillow.

- You can't seem to fall asleep.
- You fall asleep quickly but wake in the middle of the night and can't get back to sleep.
- The skin of the cuticles around the base of your fingernails becomes raw and red.

This matter of rest is something runners don't tend to discuss. In the late 1980s and early 1990s when I was running in Death Valley on a fairly regular basis, it was reassuring to discuss the importance of taking time off (especially for the heat-stressed body) with Marshall Ulrich, who was repeatedly a champion on the Death Valley/Mt. Whitney course. He was the first runner to do a quad run on the course: a double out-and-back, roughly 600 miles (966 km). Marsh is also quite the mountaineer. He's reached the summit of the highest peak on each of the seven continents.

I asked him to summarize his take on maximizing rest, especially during the off-season. Here is what he wrote:

Most runners know enough to take at least one rest day—a day with no training—each week. But, a lot of runners don't rest for a part of the year; that is, they don't allow themselves an off-season. I think this is a mistake. I've been running for over 30 years and have learned the importance of having an off-season. I believe that rest during the off-season is as beneficial as training is during the running season.

When I started running in the late 1970s, I would begin to taper my training at the end of August, after completing the Pikes Peak Marathon, which was a tradition for me for almost a decade. I backed off on my weekly miles significantly, ran more for fun than for training, and wouldn't do any racing at all until February. Typically for two months— either November and December or December and January—I wouldn't run at all. Not a step. This true off-season, off from racing and off from running, was imperative for several reasons:

1. It gave me—my body, mind, and spirit—a break.

2. It allowed me to spend more time with my family (I was married and raising three kids).

3. It provided me more time to focus on work (I was running my own business).

Now, I didn't just lie around and stuff myself with turkey and Christmas cookies, although I did indulge a little bit. My business, processing dead cattle for pet food (I called myself a used cow dealer) and processing hides for leather, requires some seriously hard physical labor, and I relished the opportunity to help my employees during the busy winter months. Throwing 50- and 100-pound (23 and 45 kg) hides

onto a pile, scooping up and spreading a shovel-full of salt, topped by another hide, followed by more salt, for at least an hour a day, is good cross-training (although the term hadn't yet been invented), especially for the upper body. It's a good cardiovascular workout, too. So, while continuing to stay fit, I gave myself a break from running.

I did my first ultra in 1983 and really started to run competitively at ultra distances in 1987. To do this, I had to increase my training miles accordingly. For about 15 years I trained over 2,000 miles (3,218 km) and raced another 1,000 miles (1,609 km) a year, including dozens of ultras and usually at least one expedition-length (at least 350 miles, or 563 kilometers) adventure race each year. During this phase of my career, rest during the off-season was even more imperative. I found I looked forward to the time off, a welcome break in the action. Physically, my legs would become fresh again. Mentally, I found that after a couple of months off, I was hungry to start running again and my competitive spirit was restored.

There have been a few years during my career when I didn't take my own best advice, and I continued to train throughout the year: once for two years in a row and, most recently, for a full year leading up to my transcontinental run in 2008. I found it mentally draining and physically damaging. My legs became fatigued, and my heart was just not into running anymore. I would have to force myself out the door. Running became a labor, and not a labor of love. That's not how it is supposed to be.

During my running career I've seen many of my friends and fellow runners continue to train year-round, and suffer for it. Some have burned out, losing their hunger for running and competition. Some have been plagued with injuries, a few even crippling themselves to the extent that they were forced out of running. Of course, rest during the off-season is likely only one part of the equation to longevity in running. Genetics also plays a significant role: how will your cartilage hold up, or how much arthritis are you likely to suffer from? I've been blessed with good genetics, which I supplement by resting during the off-season.

I'm not alone in thinking that rest is beneficial. A few years ago I was privileged to have lunch with Yiannis Kouros, who holds over 150 world records for distances from 100 to 1,300 miles (160 to 2,092 km). He has no equal in the sport of ultrarunning. As our conversation turned to rest, he affirmed that he, too, would take a month or two off during the year in which he would concentrate on his music, poetry, and painting. He said that it was a welcome relief and something that he looked forward to, because it restored his competitive spirit and brought him full circle during the year.

Everyone is unique. For some, a little rest goes a long way; for others, more rest is better. Give your body and mind a chance to heal, refresh, and grow. Be confident that cross-training will keep you fit during the off-season. When the time to start training for running arrives, you'll be ready mentally and physically. Find that perfect balance of training and time off. Listen and tune in to your body, your mind, and your spirit, and you will find the perfect balance of training and rest.

That approach has certainly worked well for Marsh over the years. Trust your body to know when and if it has managed to get enough sleep—or too much. Take note the next time you literally leap out of bed, ready to take control of the day. When that happens, you've gotten adequate sleep.

For Your Consideration

- Taking a rest day is not going to ruin your running career. Even your car usually gets the weekend off from the usual commute.

- Don't get a case of the guilts because you occasionally take a day to do nothing of an aerobic nature. Even God rested after six days of work. Hey, I'm an agnostic, but even I think that makes a lot of sense: God had an excellent sense of pacing. After inventing the human race, I'd need a day of rest, too.

- Schedule rest days into your ambitious schedule or your body will schedule them for you by translating injured days into nonscheduled rest days.

- Active rest, if it is gentle, works to some extent, although an occasional day off when you do absolutely nothing is a real tank-filler.

- Occasionally taking several days off during a single week will not greatly weaken you as long as you keep the hard/easy cycle going with your regular workouts. Without easy days and rest days, you won't be having too many hard, satisfying days in your future.

chapter

17

Wojciech Gajda/fotolia.com

RUN ALONE

*T*he loneliness of the long-distance runner. For a generation of runners, the title of Alan Sillitoe's novel of juvenile rebellion described and defined the person, usually male, who ran long distances over hill and dale or ghosted along lonely roads at any time of the day and sometimes at night, but always at least once every day and sometimes more often than that.

He (and he was almost always a "he") was a solitary figure, a loner, a sort of malcontent crossed with a misanthrope, running very much to his own drummer, very much outside the mainstream, perhaps verging on madness. He was not good at the ball sports, had little eye–hand coordination (but could leap over roots and rocks like a panther), was dark and moody, kept a low profile in school, got good grades, read so much he found it necessary to wear glasses (usually of the Clark Kent style), and had only one or two friends . . . who were usually considered losers just like he was.

This stereotype was cemented and repeated as though it were undisputed fact: that long-distance runners were introverts, antisocial, prone to long periods of silence. And all of them came from the same antisocial, boring, nerdy mold.

Of course, it wasn't really true . . . except in those cases when it *was* true—when a long-distance runner was actually introverted, antisocial, and prone to long periods of time where he kept his mouth closed (except to breathe) and his opinions to himself and eschewed the company of others with great enthusiasm.

In reality, most of the long-distance runners of the 1970s and 1980s were sociable enough. Some 80,000 of them used to get together one day a year in May to run the Bay-to-Breakers race in San Francisco. Marathons grew large enough to boast tens of thousands of participants. Running clubs cropped up in every big city and many small towns, and they were populated with people sociable enough that they managed to attract other like-minded (and like-bodied) people to their ranks. In fact, today there are more than 1,000 running clubs in the Road Runners Club of America.

Runners, it seems, *were* sociable; they went to great pains to seek out other runners. And once women became involved in larger numbers, running became more sociable still as women brought their often social personalities and skills to the sport and lifestyle. In many instances, women would not run at all if they could not run with their women friends. From a social standpoint, running provides a wonderful common ground for groups of women, and the fitness aspect is a terrific bonus.

The Greater Boston Track Club in the late 1970s and early 1980s sported a dozen or so national-class runners who worked out together. Women's running groups formed up for Saturday morning runs.

Corporate competition brought together disparate employees all inter-mixing and proudly sporting the logo of their company, warehouse-woman striding out with the marketing VP.

More recently, the tendency of people to train and race together has further escalated. There are charity running groups and computer-gener-ated virtual training groups, often tied in with major races. Everybody's running with somebody.

The solitary runner backlit against the rising sun on the far horizon has become a rarity.

The days of a runner like 1960s marathon world record–holder Derek Clayton running hard workouts day after day while avoiding other run-ners is nearly gone. Of course, Clayton usually ran alone not for spiritual renewal, but because he didn't want to let his competitors know what kind of workouts he was doing.

Clayton *did* enjoy running with other runners in races. His personality seemed to be defined by an admission he shared: "I love to have some-body next to me at 15 miles, so I can grind them into the ground." (No wonder he spent so much time running alone. He'd have had trouble finding someone to run with if that person were going to get ground into the ground.)

We could all use some alone space and time—some quality Thoreau moments that Derek Clayton would not appreciate because of his com-petitive nature, especially these days when we are bombarded with com-munications of all sorts all the time. We are literally being smothered by communications, drowned in talk and text. Yet in spite of all the yakking, it's the rare conversation that is truly riveting and memorable. In fact, conversation is becoming a lost art, killed off by blogging and mortally wounded by text messaging. Gone the way of the reel-to-reel tape recorder.

To attempt to escape the constant babble is to court sanity.

A solitary run can provide that escape and that sanity and in the process is a thing of beauty on two important fronts:

1. Become reacquainted with yourself.
2. It offers an opportunity for play.

First of all, it gets you away from the distractions of daily life and encourages you to meet yourself and to become reacquainted with the you that is lost and lonely in the fog of white noise. Many people these days seem adrift from themselves, unable or unwilling to examine themselves and work toward a fuller realization of the athletic potential trapped within. They would do better to schedule some quality time with themselves instead of surrounding themselves with the furry and too-comfortable coat of oblivion.

We all need some time away, some time alone. Some people are able to create this personal time even in the middle of a bustling city surrounded by thousands of people and hundreds of distractions. Others can't, but they have learned that they can achieve the quiet time by running away for an hour or two.

When you voluntarily strip yourself of all distractions and distortions, you are, for the duration of the run, free from the life perpetrated on you by a world panting for your attention. No phone calls. No instant messaging. No lists of what's "in" or "out." No brand names vying for your attention and your dollar. No badgering or begging or cajoling or nudging. No headphones cutting you off from the real world around you—the world where birds chirp and where your breathing is an umbilical cord that connects you to the heart of the world.

Running on your own offers the advantage of developing hard discipline of body and mind. It takes a great deal of motivation to head out on a long run alone. It involves a commitment of focus and hard work . . . and usually the acceptance of the various ups and downs you have come to associate with running long. It is, in essence, the training version of Alberto Salazar's famous statement that at the starting line, we are all cowards. The very fact that we go out the door alone to face the potential obstacles of the long run makes us better runners. For most of us, the most ferocious enemy we face in our lifetime is ourselves, because we know all of our moves and countermoves, all of our excuses and rationalizations.

Running alone builds physical and mental strength and perseverance.

It also offers an opportunity to play with a run. When you run with a group, you are stuck either following the dictates of the group leader or held down by the speed—or lack of speed—of the slowest runner in the group. When you are alone, there are no such dictates. You can speed up or slow down or throw in a few extra hills if you think they will help improve your fitness . . . or perhaps just because there is a particularly attractive hill along the route. There is no better way to do fartlek than by running alone.

Running with a group is desirable when doing especially long runs because the group creates a distraction so that the long run seems to go by easier and faster. But when you run a race, even if it is among a throng of thousands, your race is your own. You are running within yourself, and if you don't occasionally go out alone, you will not have learned how to confront your weaknesses at stressful times during the race.

Approaching a considerable hill on a workout, I tend to blanch a bit as I approach it, anticipating the work ahead. Running hills alone, over a period of weeks, I can increase the rhythm of my breathing going into the hills, getting a jump on the increased respiration I'm going to need.

In a group run, I can feel pulled along; alone, I'm stripped bare and faced with exactly how I handle the hill versus how I know I want to handle it.

Running alone for a long run can have its disadvantages, however. If you are in decent shape and you're running a 16-mile workout, you may have a tendency, once you're warmed up, to daydream, to disassociate, and to just drift along while your mind wanders. In a group run, your mind doesn't tend to wander because there is always something going on (often the most talkative people weaving long stories or rattling off jokes).

If you can do a long run alone and keep your focus and concentration piqued, monitoring your body functions as you go, you can greatly improve your ability to race well. Without the distraction of the group, you can more easily learn to monitor your breathing, your energy output, your running form, the slap of your shoes on the asphalt, and your overall performance. If you hit a rough spot while you're alone, you can run through it and come out the other side a much stronger runner, much more self-reliant and confident.

Running alone, you spend quality time with yourself, rocked gently by the in and out of your breath and the beat of your heart and the sigh of the world around you. You are in sync with the basic rhythm and beat of your own body and of the cosmos of which you are a molecule.

All things extraneous are stripped away. All complexities become simple—and accessible.

When you are pounded and confused 24/7 by a myriad of questions demanding answers and decisions needing making, all of them hyper-charged and demanding an instant answer (no matter how pressingly important or merely trivial, there is no distinction), your body and mind stumble and become misaligned. Stripped on the solitary run of that constant assault of the senses, rolling along a quiet country road or a pathway in a park, your breath coming regularly and strongly, your mind can click into a primal dragon gear. Quickly and confidently it can sort through the dozens of questions and problems that have stymied you. Like a computer alphabetizing a database, your mind can line up the questions in a remarkably logical way, bringing only one topic forward at a time, stripping it of its nettles and disguises until it stands before you, stark and vulnerable and easily dealt with. The question that has dogged you for three days is solved in three miles. You shake your head at how absolutely simple it was—once the extraneous camouflage was shunted off to the nowhere where it belongs.

When we are out on that endless road or that path to nowhere, we are also open to experience the connection to a greater whole. This is not an experience that needs to be too closely examined or pigeonholed as a religious experience. On a long run alone, the experience is available

to the faithful as well as to the faithless. That serenity seeps not from our running legs into the earth, but the other way around: It comes up from the earth as it makes us one with the environment through which we move, as it refreshes and fuels that spiritual tank in all of us that we so badly want to fill. It is only filled, though, when we are quiet and with ourselves, and when we are comfortable with the quiet around us and within us.

OK, so that sounds just about as New Age hokey as you can get. Trust me, New Age I ain't. Think back to long runs you did alone that are memorable even years later. I can think of one that is more than 20 years old: an 18-miler (29 km) on a Saturday morning after an overnight storm that knocked out the power, broke tree limbs off century-old trees, and made a shambles of the neighborhood. The run wasn't easy, and it wasn't through a redwood forest. It was through a suburban area, along what was usually a well-traveled road, and it involved vaulting twisted and broken tree limbs. It was cold and it was wet and it was windy. For a couple of hours I had the whole world to myself, except for the occasional confused dog wandering around wondering what had happened to its orderly world, and utility repair crews that were trying to reinstitute the order on which those dogs depended for their sanity.

Gas stations post signs warning motorists not to top off their tanks for fear of overflowing. Well, that 18-mile run overfilled my spiritual and psychological tanks to the point of near-ecstatic excess. That run was so good that it's difficult, these long years later, to even classify it as a run. It was an entirely unique experience. And it was an experience that would have been denied had I done the run with anyone else (not that anyone else would have volunteered to venture out into the ravaged streets).

When you run alone, the pace you run at any one time is always the pace *you* choose. Do you want to pick it up to the next lamppost? Do you want to cruise over the next mile? Do you have an urge to turn off the road you usually run to explore a neighborhood you've never experienced before?

You need ask no one for permission.

You need only give in to your own whim.

You are, for that precious time, captain of your own ship. And for that time, your ship—inside and out—is improved by its customization of momentarily self-centered physicality. You become the animal you were meant to be, and by that act, you are one with what is real, not with what is virtual.

You are once more renewed by a sacrament of sweat, a process you can only accomplish solo, in a sport in which even in the middle of a 10,000-entrant race, you are ultimately alone.

But far from lonely.

For Your Consideration

- Perform an experiment. Chuck the iPod and the GPS, the hydration pack and the heart-rate monitor and go on a solo run. Listen to your own breathing and absorb the world through which you glide. When did you last meet up with yourself out on the open road?

- No matter how often you run and train with others, set at least one run a week aside just for yourself.

- On a solo run, explore a new course. Make sure it is a safe course by checking it out on a map or with people who are familiar with the area. Make it your own.

- On a trip to a new area, ask the person at the front desk of your hotel if there is a running route that will give you a tour of the most interesting sights in your new environment.

- Next time you visit the town or city where you grew up, run some of the routes of your childhood. What's changed? What hasn't? Do your childhood haunts seem incredibly small compared to your expanded world of adulthood?

- When you do a long run alone, give in to your urges to wander off the beaten path. Throw in an extra hill or a detour down a street you haven't explored before.

- On your next solo long run, practice keeping your focus on monitoring the performance of your systems for the entire run. Don't allow your mind to wander. This will make the workout doubly effective.

AP Photo

RUN TOGETHER

with

Bill Rodgers

Whenever and wherever we run and race, we do so alone, whether we're on a run with friends or surrounded by 30,000 strangers at a big-city marathon event.

Our run is done both within and without ourselves simultaneously. It is generated by us and us alone, and we are wholly responsible for it and one with it.

Because running long distance is a sport and a lifestyle we ultimately do alone, naked to the world, it holds a special place among human activities while also demanding a special kind of commitment.

In most sports and human activities, we are not so alone, so "out there." Our shortcomings in performing various activities—from exercising and competing to completing work on the job—can be at least partially covered by friends and teammates who can run interference when we are having a bad day.

On a football team, a pair of linemen can open a delicious hole in the line for a fullback who is not the most agile or fastest man in the backfield. In the military, a particularly good shot can cover the back of a quick and agile infantryman who is the company's worst shot but best stealth point man. At a sales meeting, the best presenter may not be the most organized person on the team, but backed by those who are better organized, can give one outrageously winning presentation.

It's called teamwork, and it has worked for tens of thousands of years. It accounts in large part for the fact that the human race is still around and dominant in the world. It is also what makes the team, from a strictly numbers standpoint, consistently stronger than the average person within the team.

Is teamwork applicable to running?

Certainly. It's what makes what is ultimately an "alone" (but not lonely) sport so attractive to many people who hate to be alone.

Teamwork is involved in marathon relay teams, in Hood-to-Coast relay teams, in corporate road race teams, in club or corporate track and field teams, and in clubs participating in running events.

Although each runner ultimately runs alone and is responsible for his or her success or failure, running with others has a special allure in the world of sports.

Running with others creates an environment in which the status and caste system of the everyday world is chucked, the civilized world's uniforms are left in the locker room, and everyone shows up for the Thursday evening track workout in shorts and a T-shirt. Stripped for action, you can gravitate to people in the group who share your 400-meter repeat potential rather than your rung on the corporate ladder.

Running with others creates an environment in which lifelong friendships are created based on a common love of movement and the strip-

ping away of pretense. People who have little in common otherwise run together step for step, mile after mile, year after year.

Running with others is for some the most important motivating force to get out the door. For some people, that first step is the most difficult, but when they know they're obliged to meet others to go for that daily or weekly run, there is a motivation at work that goes beyond mere guilt at letting the group down. For some, the lack of a group would keep them from running.

Running in groups is especially attractive to female runners. Although male runners seem OK running alone (as do many female runners), women tend to like to get together in groups to train and race. Some women admit that if it weren't for their running group they doubt they could stay motivated to run. Female running groups have certainly paid off. In some road races (the Portland, Oregon, marathon, for one), women outnumber men, a reality that would have been unthinkable as recently as the 1980s. The phenomenon of women outnumbering men in road races began emerging early in Canada, beginning in the mid-1990s.

Colleges and running shops sometimes host classes or training workshops for local runners. Participants in these groups tend to stick together as training partners after the classes or workshops are over.

Running with others, especially on particularly hard or long runs and in races, creates a special bond that has few comparisons. This bond is based on the following:

1. Misery loves company. On particularly long or difficult workouts or challenging races, it is always good to have along a friendly ear to listen to your whining, moaning, and complaining. Afterward, you can share the high and low points of the run or race. Let's face it: There is a particularly perverted side of human nature that better remembers the outrageously horrible than the sublime, and wallows in the retelling of it.

2. Life as shared meaning. On runs or races that are going as expected, the distance always seems shorter and the experience more meaningful in the company of a friend or two . . . or three. At the heart of every shared running experience are several miles that seem forged in heaven, where the asphalt is softer, the wind always a tailwind, and the breathing always under control. To imagine having the same experience running that particular run alone is to court a fantasy.

3. Energy exchange. The metaphysical and the mystical can come together during a particularly long run or an especially challenging race when three or four runners who train together regularly

pass energy back and forth to each other as the need arises. This may sound way too New Age to most people, but when one person begins to falter or hits an ugly patch, the rest of the group can pass energy to that person. This exchange can be so palpable that the needy runner is often compelled to comment on the phenomenon. I can recall even today the San Francisco Marathon of 1978 when Larry Tunis and I paced our friend Bill Howard through his first marathon. Out along the Great Highway, more than 20 miles into the race, Bill began to falter. Larry and I rolled up beside him, and within a few more strides, Bill commented on how he was picking up needed energy from the two of us. It's as close to sharing a responsibility for someone else's run as it's possible to get in an activity in which we all ultimately participate alone.

Running with others better than ourselves, even if briefly, can have tremendously positive consequences. If you always run with people equal to or weaker than you are, you'll never improve (which is an argument against national-class runners picking only races they know they have a chance of winning). If you run with people better than you are, your striving to stay with them, even if for only a few miles, will improve your running.

Years ago, several of us at *Runner's World* who wanted to improve would go out for a few miles to get warmed up and then meet up with some of the stud runners who worked at Starting Line Sports (a retail outlet owned by *Runner's World*) and who were former aggies from UC-Davis—guys like Angel Martinez and Peanut Harms. We knew we couldn't keep up with them for their entire workout, but they weren't yet warmed up and we were, so we could manage to hold on for the first few miles and learn to run, at least briefly, with the big dogs.

Bill Rodgers, four-time winner of the Boston and New York Marathons, used to offer the same opportunity to visiting runners when he had his Cleveland Circle store along the Boston Marathon course. If you were a 46-minute 10K runner and you were in town and you wanted to run the first several miles of Bill's afternoon workout, he'd be happy to take you along for a few miles while he warmed up. Of course, once he was warmed up and shifted to ever-higher gears, you were pretty much on your own.

What made the Greater Boston Track Club (GBTC) such a force in the late 1970s and early 1980s was that they had a dozen members who were similar in talent. Whoever was feeling his oats that day would pull the others along with him. Runners such as Bob Hodge, Randy Thomas, Vin Fleming, Greg Meyer, and Dick Mahoney were so potent singly and as a team because they pushed each other and in the process became better.

It is the rare long-distance runner who is capable of improving while running in a vacuum. Emil Zatopek (Czechoslovakia), Derek Clayton (Australia), and Jerome Drayton (Canada) come to mind as exceptions.

The benefits of running in a group were overlooked for a time. In the 1970s geographically specific running groups were common. Besides the aforementioned GBTC, the most famous long-distance running group was centered in the Gainesville, Florida, area and boasted runners such as Frank Shorter, Jack Bacheler, Jeff Galloway, John Parker (author of *Once a Runner*), and others.

From the mid-1980s onward, the concept of the running group fell by the wayside, but over the past few years it has reemerged, and to good effect.

Groups such as the Hanson brothers' group in Michigan, Alberto Salazar's group in Beaverton, Oregon, and perhaps most famously, the Mammoth Lakes group (Deena Kastor, Meb Keflezighi, Ryan Hall, and others) have all contributed to forming a much deeper pool of talent in the United States, and it's promoted a real team sense among the various groups.

Although we run every run alone when it comes right down to it, running is one of the rare occasions in life in which we can be alone together.

In August of 1980 I spent a week with Bill Rodgers in Boston while working on a major feature on him for *Runner's World*. At the time, Bill was considered the King of the Roads. He easily dominated the road-racing scene, at one point winning more than 20 road races in a row, everything from the 5K to the marathon. He would ultimately win four Boston Marathons and four New York City Marathons. During that visit, he was not in a terribly good mood. At the height of his prowess as a runner, President Jimmy Carter had announced that the United States would boycott the Moscow Olympic Games. Bill's best chance to medal in the marathon had been snatched away.

On one of the days during the visit, we went to the track where a half-dozen other members of the Greater Boston Track Club joined Bill for their weekly repeat workouts. It was hot and muggy, but they ran repeat after repeat, seemingly enjoying the process.

As I worked on this chapter, that day came back to me vividly. I contacted Bill to ask him to comment on the special relationship that develops when a group of runners trains together. He sent along this mini-memoir of those special relationships:

> *When I think of some of the reasons I love running, it is clear that maybe key for me has been that the social/friendship aspect has been paramount. This became very clear to me as a 15-year-old Newington,*

Connecticut, high school sophomore when I joined our cross-country team with my brother Charlie and good childhood friend Jason. In fact, that first year we were almost the whole team! I still remember us recruiting some friends, including a smoker and a basketball player who I think lasted one race.

But most profoundly, I remember our new coach, Frank O'Rourke, who'd been a track athlete at Boston University and who quickly reenergized our team spirit with consistent support and sensible workouts. Soon we were a force.

When we won our conference title, we ran through the season with that banner of success. I don't think too many people paid us much attention, but we were stoked. My senior year in cross-country, our team was stunned by the appearance of NHS cheerleaders at our meets—at a cross-country meet! We had gained some clout.

In college with Amby Burfoot and Jeff Galloway at Wesleyan University, a Division III school, we had another wizard of a coach, Elmer Swanson, a man who knew instinctively to keep us focused and let us explore our strengths gradually. We bonded as a team and are still close today, more than 40 years later.

I still recall that feeling of intensity cheering on your teammates during races in track and cross-country, something lacking in road running. On the other hand, I made so many friends through this sport, and it seems like this will never change.

In my middle 20s I joined the GBTC [Greater Boston Track Club], as did a bunch of guys I knew and sometimes trained with. Again, a charismatic high-energy coach led the way, Coach Billy Squires. As a former near-four-minute-miler in the 1950s at Notre Dame, he had credibility. But what counted was that he lifted us up—all of us on the team—and we lifted each other up in big training groups that occasionally degenerated into outright races as we raced for home. I can still hear Greg Meyer making wisecracks, Coach Squires speaking in a strange Boston accent and becoming near-hysterical with his determination on behalf of our athletes at races, and all of us knowing we were pretty darned good. That high was something else, especially because we all knew we had helped each other get there.

I can still remember one of my last 20-mile workouts leading up to Boston that I did with three or four friends. My Brit friend Dave Oliver called it the Novocain Run. It was 8 °F (−13 °C), but we did it, laughed about how cold it was, and believe me, we would not have done it alone! We cheered each other on, trying to beat each other, broke bread together, had a beer or two, listened to music, and ran absolutely everywhere on this planet together. Nothing could stop us except God himself, and I like to think that as we went by he saluted us, because

he made us the running animals that we are—and the friends that we'll always be.

The benefits of running with others can't be overstressed. The playful competition among friends can profoundly improve your running skills, and the friendships tend to span the years in a way that casual friendships never do.

For Your Consideration

- Once a week, seek out a running group that is a tier above your talents, and after warming up for a few miles, set out with them at their pace during their warm-up phase. When you are dropped as they pick up the pace, head off to complete your own workout.

- Find a running partner who is roughly at your level and run with him or her once a week on a tempo or fartlek session. Take turns throwing in the surges and picking up the pace, but don't attempt to blow the other runner's doors off. Cooperate with each other so both of you improve.

- Find one or two runners who are a tier below you and spend one workout a week running with them at their pace. It will slow you down some and force you to take an easy day, and in the process you can share with them some of the lessons you've learned over the years.

- Run with a half-dozen other runners of roughly the same talent and form a line. As you run along comfortably, have the person at the back of the line come forward and set the pace at the front for five minutes. Then have the person at the end of the line come forward and do the same.

- Schedule one evening a week for group track workouts. Break into groups of equal or near-equal talent, and pump out your speed workout for the week. The time on speed workouts and on long runs always goes by faster if you are doing it with other runners. Then head out to the local pizza parlor to refill your carbo tanks.

JOIN A CLUB

Let's make this simple and put it right up front for runners who love to run on the roads: www.rrca.org. That's the home page of the Road Runners Club of America, the largest and most active amalgamation of running clubs in the world, and the backbone and protector of road races and road racers in the United States. The RRCA turned 50 years old in 2008. It has a membership of 200,000 runners who are active in more than 1,000 running clubs.

Now, just for fun, let's also throw out there the Hash House Harriers, the naughty but nice running club that has chapters throughout the world, and in some of the most out-of-the-way places in the world, including two chapters in the Antarctic. The HHH's central Web site is www.gthhh.com. The Harriers claim to have 18,626 members in more than 1700 "kennels" spread across 178 countries, and who's to argue with a club whose male members sometimes dress up in red dresses and then go outside to race?

We'll discuss these two unique clubs a little later, but first let's talk about running clubs in general.

Real runners, the anaerobic athletic artists, ran on tracks under the supervision of, at first, the Amateur Athletic Union, or AAU (an umbrella organization covering all amateur sports), and eventually, once track and field was separated from the other amateur sports, the USATF (USA Track & Field).

There was the odd blue-collar sportsman or confused collegiate guy who ran along the roads, but they weren't part of the official world of runners. They were oddballs, sometimes referred to as "ham and eggers," who once a year at Boston got together and ran a marathon. The numbers at Boston for its first 75 years were no threat to the AAU. In 1910, for instance, there were 169 entrants; in 1946 there were 112. There were a number of road races of varying distances, especially in New England and on the West Coast, but the fields were universally small and frequently consisted of the same two or three dozen runners. (In his research for a story on the founding of the RRCA, Hal Higdon discovered that in 1958 there were eight marathons in the United States; today there are more than 400.)

Elite sporting clubs catered to the upper crust of society. The Boston Athletic Association had its own elaborate clubhouse and facilities to support everything from swimming to bowling; it even sported a wine cellar. Clubs like the BAA supplied the athletes for the revival of the Olympic Games in 1896.

There were also the vanguard clubs such as the New York Pioneer Club, which was formed as an all-inclusive, integrated track club. It was formed a decade before Jackie Robinson was signed by the Dodgers, and welcomed Jews and African Americans, the most famous of the latter

being Ted Corbitt, the grandfather of U.S. ultramarathoning and one of the founders of the RRCA.

Average road runners, however, had little in the way of organizations they could join or that catered to them. They would pile into a car, go to a road race, run the road race, hang around a bit to socialize and down a beer or three with their fellow competitors, and then they'd pile back into the car and drive home.

It was a different situation in England, where sporting clubs were common and some of them had large contingents of both track and road runners.

During the 1950s the ranks of road runners in the United States began to grow, but they gained no respect among the track and field types, who still saw themselves as the pure runners and elite athletes. (Let's face it: They had history on their side. The first ancient Greek Olympics featured only one event: a 200-meter sprint race inside a stadium.)

The AAU began to hound the growing number of road runners for membership dues and went so far as to require an AAU card for participation in some road events the organization had in the past ignored. None of the membership dues went toward providing any services for road runners, and many road runners simply refused to pay for the privilege of receiving nothing in return.

It was into that growing vacuum that the Road Runners Club of American stepped.

To quote the history of the RRCA from its website: "In the 1950s there were very few opportunities for runners to train and compete after college. In the August 1957 issue of *The Long Distance Log* an editorial by Olympian H. Browning Ross proposed to develop an organization for American distance runners. The concept was modeled after the Road Runners Club of the United Kingdom founded in 1952. . . . At a February 22, 1958, meeting at the Paramount Hotel in New York City, Ross and nine others discussed the general direction for the organization and developed the basic operating structure."

The founders of the RRCA wanted a countrywide organization to oversee their activities and to provide a roof under which they could pursue their ambitions.

The Hash House Harriers, on the other hand, date back to before the RRCA and are a bit less organized . . . and proud of it. They formed in Kuala Lumpur, Malaysia, in 1938 when some British colonial officials and expatriots got together after work on Monday evenings to go for a run. One runner (the "hare") would go out and leave a paper trail that the other runners (the hounds) would then follow. Afterward, the runners would hang around, drink beer, and swap stories. The HHH (or H3) has been known for decades as "a drinking club with a running problem."

They frequently put on outrageous races, including the tradition of staging an annual Red Dress Run (http://reddress.gotothehash.net/), where frequently members of both genders run the event wearing a red dress. (Seeing a mustached, hairy-legged guy running down the street in a red dress can be very disconcerting.)

Most running clubs, of course, are more traditional, and in fact, without them and their members and their organizational skill, most of the decent road races in this country would vanish.

Clubs vary in size from a dozen members to some of giant proportions, among them the New York Road Runners (with 40,000 members) and the Atlanta Track Club (9,000 members). The NYRR's premiere road racing event is, of course, the New York City Marathon, and the ATC's is the July 4th Peachtree 10K.

What are the advantages of joining a running club? Whereas a half-century ago, most road runners practiced their sport alone, today's long-distance runner is typically more of a social being, and often actually depends on the motivation of fellow runners to get in the miles needed to race at various long distances. The essential long run, the backbone of any long-distance running program, is less painful when done with a group. Running clubs usually offer training groups at various levels, so they can benefit novice runners as well as help veteran runners improve their performances.

Clubs also provide an opportunity to give back to the sport. As already mentioned, without the dedication of running clubs, there would be very few road races available. Becoming a club member allows you to volunteer to help keep the road racing circuit alive and well—and growing.

Many clubs offer ambitious programs to encourage youngsters to take up running, and in that way help ameliorate the vacuum left in youth fitness with the demise of so many physical education programs in the schools. Some clubs (including the RRCA) have even begun to offer dating services for runners with common interests beyond running.

A growing number of professionally run road races are looking to hire experienced race organizers. One of the best ways to get that necessary experience is by joining a club and working on its race committees. Some clubs, in fact, are large enough that they have salaried race officials.

Many running clubs are eager to subsidize local charities; if you're involved with a local charity and want to build a bridge to contributors, joining the local running club would provide a means to do that.

Many clubs publish their own magazines or newsletters and maintain Web sites where you can learn about publications or Web communities, or offer your talents if you are proficient in writing, editing, or design. (The RRCA has an annual awards banquet at their convention honoring the best publications and Web sites in various club size categories.)

In periods of economic uncertainty, running clubs offer all sorts of networking opportunities for jobs and for promoting your business, both through the club membership and through businesses affiliated with the club. Such applications, of course, need to be done tastefully and sensitively.

Clubs also provide ready access to better runners and experienced coaches who can give valuable and solid training advice. This is especially beneficial for the novice runner who may otherwise go by the wayside because of confusion, frustration, or lack of improvement.

Clubs also frequently put together trips to out-of-town races; because they enter as a group, they can offer considerable savings for individual members. They also charter planes and buses and organize carpools to go to races.

Of course the most valuable commodity a club provides is that element you can't put a price on, camaraderie. Any activity is more fun when you're doing it with a group of like-minded people.

For Your Consideration

- Join a running club for both social and practical reasons.
- Running clubs provide ready access to coaches and training programs.
- Running clubs frequently organize social events that provide ready entry into the running world for those folks who are socially shy and retiring.
- By joining a running club and volunteering to help out, you can give something back to the sport and thereby keep it healthy. A lot of the folks who volunteer all the time can use a little time off so they don't burn out.
- Self-conscious newcomers to running can find comfort running within a group structure. This has been especially true over the past decade with women entering running without previous athletic experience. The club systems are extremely supportive of new runners.

VOLUNTEER

with

Allan Steinfeld

Long-distance runners make outstanding volunteers, primarily because being a good long-distance runner requires that you be obsessive about training while also dependable and responsible in numerous aspects of life.

Let me give you two examples: *Marathon & Beyond* magazine carries a feature each issue titled "My Most Unforgettable Marathon (And What I Learned from It)." A marathoner relates his or her most memorable marathon and explains the lessons learned from it. The feature has been carried each issue since the magazine's inception in January of 1997.

In the November/December 2009 issue, Lisa Garrone of New York City didn't write one of the regular "Most Unforgettable" installments, but she did a feature that she titled "A Different Kind of Unforgettable Marathon." A member of the New York Road Runners club and a veteran of its annual marathon, Lisa volunteered to help at the race in early November. Let's let her explain:

> I would like to say that I decided to volunteer to give back. Certainly, that was a big part of it. After all, I had run 30 marathons in 20 states and four countries. I surely owed something somewhere, and then some. Volunteering is also a new requirement for runners hoping to qualify for the NYC Marathon based on the number of local races they run. But I had already deferred my guaranteed entry from this year and therefore had a guaranteed entry next year.
>
> The truth is, much like my first NYC Marathon eight years earlier, I was attracted by the idea of how glorious it would be to participate and to do well. I thought about how many times I had been handed a sports drink that was mixed incorrectly or had found a station that had run out of water at the worst time. *Not on my watch*, I thought. Literally, I was an experienced runner. I would make the ideal volunteer because I knew what it was like to be on the receiving end of a water cup. I was going to do it right.

And do it right, she did. She strove to be the perfect volunteer, and for all intents and purposes, she was. Except for the fact that she had not anticipated the repetitive nature of handing cup after cup after cup of water for hour after hour using the same arm motion, which literally wore her down. She was one of the last volunteers to leave her station. She wrote:

> . . . as I jogged toward the nearest subway station, aching from the standing and cheering and the holding, I could already feel my resolve strengthening. Next time, I would do arm exercises to

strengthen my water arm. I could practice my pouring technique in my kitchen. Stretching lower tendons before cup crushing would help. Maybe [and here comes her marathoner's competitive streak] next year, our water station could be ready even further ahead of the other teams. Visions of future volunteering PRs danced in my head. Much like after running my first marathon, I was humbled by the experience of volunteering. But, just like after my first marathon, I loved it and was determined to do it again."

In the March/April 2010 issue of the *Marathon & Beyond*, Ellen Lyons wrote an installment of "My Most Unforgettable Marathon" about the 2009 Boston Marathon. A veteran of nine Boston Marathons and a local, Ellen didn't run in 2009—she volunteered because she was injured. After nearly a decade of running Boston, this time she was going to do it differently.

Ellen spent the day with several other volunteers organizing sweat bags for a group of police officers who were running the marathon. Her two fellow volunteers are members of the LAPD, and as you might imagine, the three of them are organizational mavens. They set up the bags in rows based on the race numbers of their owners. They got done fast enough that they had time to duck outside and catch the women's finish. Ellen wrote: "The women's finish is inspiring, even with Kara Goucher taking third place. I rarely have a chance to appreciate long-distance running as a sport, and the top women's performances make me proud—I'm lucky to be a runner, an athlete."

Ellen put in a long day but a satisfying one. She ended her article this way: "Much later, it is getting dark—the sky now reversed, carbon-paper clouds and pink streaks waning. I am parking the car, walking across my lawn to my door, limping a little, sore and proud—feeling very much as though I had participated in the Boston Marathon, despite my lack of tinfoil blanket and medal. My neighbor Al yells to me: 'Hey, Ellen! How did you do?' I call back to him, explaining that I didn't run. He doesn't hear me. 'Congratulations!' he yells. 'You'll sleep well tonight!' I decide not to explain any further. Al is right: I will sleep well tonight."

It is no exaggeration to state that very little would get done in the world if all the world's volunteers were abducted by an alien spacecraft. Certainly in running, entry fees don't come close to covering the cost of putting on a race even with volunteers; without volunteers, race entry fees would soar and running races as we know them would vanish from the face of the earth, as would charity events of all kinds.

Volunteers are essential to the survival of most events. As we've seen with so many natural calamities, without volunteer help, fatalities would be multiplied several times.

Fortunately, volunteering is its own unique reward.

Fortunately, volunteers who have never run a step, step forward to help put on running races.

At the Napa Valley Marathon (32 years old in 2010), volunteers from Calistoga (the little resort town where the race starts) are responsible for the first seven miles of the course. Some intersections have been staffed and monitored by the same families since the race began. Families pass their intersections down from generation to generation. These are family affairs, and woe to anyone within the marathon's organizational structure who makes the mistake of trying to take their intersections away from them.

One Napa Valley volunteer worked the same intersection for more than 25 years. When he learned he had terminal cancer, his wish was to stay alive long enough to do his volunteer duties one last time—which he did.

My wife and I have been working aid stations at the grueling Western States Endurance Run for more than two decades, most of that time at the Red Star aid station at 16.5 miles.

Roughly 1,500 volunteers are needed to put on the Western States race. Many of the volunteers are on duty for two and sometimes three days straight. Lee and Diana Scott organize and run the Red Star aid station; they are not runners themselves. They come in Friday morning to set the station up, and the crew camps out at the site Friday night, before getting up at 5:00 a.m. on Saturday to get everything ready for the runners. After the station is broken down at 10:00 a.m., Lee and Diana head for the finish line at Auburn High School to staff the finish line aid station and later to set up the breakfast cafeteria, which Diana runs until the race is complete and everyone has left the course, which is on the far side of 11:00 a.m.

Some volunteers, of course, manage to both help out and run the race. That's easy enough to do if your volunteering involves pre-race-day activities: marketing the race, sending out entry forms, filing permits with government entities that need to clear the way for the race to happen, ordering supplies, and even handing out bib numbers and T-shirts the day before the race.

Some race directors manage to run their own races. One of the most energetic and ambitious of them all is Thomas Hill III, who is the primary driving force behind the Oklahoma City Memorial Marathon. On race day he runs in his own race, and one of his endearing traditions is that, well into the race, where the course passes a donut shop, he volunteers to buy a donut for any runner who can stomach one. Talk about race-day carbo-loading. Of course once he finishes, he continues to be a Tasmanian devil, rushing here and there and everywhere to hand out

prizes, check that the huge post-race party is running smoothly, and serve as the general for the whole shebang.

One of the most memorable double-duty experiences I ever had occurred in the summer of 1980 when I was working at *Runner's World* and we were putting on the annual Corporate Cup championships at Spartan Stadium at San Jose State College in California. Bob Anderson, the publisher of *Runner's World*, wanted everything to be as prim and proper as possible. So a group of us on the magazine staff served as judges of the track events. What that entailed was that we stood on a small set of bleachers on the inside of the track near the start/finish line to make sure that the contestants followed the rules and were scored properly. We wore three-piece dark-colored suits, which under the afternoon sun absorbed an enormous amount of heat.

The bleachers were specially constructed with a curtain in the back so that the inside of the bleachers could serve as a dressing room. Most of us standing in the sun scoring the races all day long were also on the *Runner's World* track team. As our events approached, we'd make an inconspicuous exit from the bleachers and slip into the "dressing room," where we'd shed the three-piece suits and—like Superman in the phone booth—change into our action uniforms. We had little time to warm up before we had to line up at the start line.

Changed into my running togs and sort of warmed up (from the blistering sun), I walked over to the start line for the mile run and realized I was standing next to Rick Wohlhuter, who'd won the bronze medal in the 800 meters at the 1972 Munich Olympics. Needless to say, my pedestrian 5:24 didn't impress him much. My sweat-drenched three-piece suit didn't impress my fellow judges much, either. The fact that the day stands out so well 30 years later speaks well of the volunteering process.

Someone who knows volunteering in all of its myriad forms is Allan Steinfeld. For many years, Allan was president of the New York Road Runners and the race director of the New York City Marathon. He had this to say about volunteering:

> *I first volunteered at Road Runners in 1975, three years before Fred [Fred Lebow, then president of the club] hired me. My reason for volunteering was that I wanted to be part of something that was healthy and good for people—which made me feel good.*
>
> *Volunteers are the lifeblood of road racing events, and without them, most races couldn't exist. The New York City Marathon has approximately 12,000 volunteers in pre-race, race, and post-race positions. They come from all walks of life, and some even get to use their professional skills, such as medical personnel and interpreters*

(which are specific to New York). It is the volunteers that the runners interact with and not the staff. We have always asked the volunteers to treat the runners as guests in their home (and not like in-laws) because they are guests in our home of New York City. When runners talk about memories of our race, they always mention the special treatment from the volunteers. It is probably the same throughout the world. The volunteers mirror the excitement and energy of the runners who come to run.

In our case, the volunteers want to be part of an exciting annual celebration of life that the city and its people embrace and is known worldwide. They want to feel good about themselves knowing that they are helping people from around the world realize their dreams. They also receive T-shirts from the event that they wear proudly to show their friends and neighbors that they were part of the marathon. When they see the smiling faces cross the finish line, they feel that their time was well-spent. It is almost as good as sex.

Just what is a volunteer, anyway? It is sometimes confusing these days, as we'll discuss. According to the *New Oxford American Dictionary*, a volunteer is "a person who freely offers to take part in an enterprise or undertake a task." In a curious oxymoron these days, there are some strange hybrid volunteers: "forced volunteers" and "paid volunteers."

I often see references to the enormous number of "volunteer" hours young people put in these days. Unfortunately, the volunteer hours they put in are not freely given. Because they are required to volunteer to graduate from high school or college, when you think of it, their service is similar to the community service required by the courts of various miscreants. Once these requirements are lifted, very few younger people willingly offer their services, unless they are paid by the organizing committee.

This is unfortunate, because volunteering freely is its own reward.

Let's return to the Napa Valley Marathon. The race has a limit of 2,300 runners. Roughly 70 medical personnel attend to the runners' medical needs, but there are precious few instances in which they are needed in their medical capacity. So they pitch in passing out cups of water and sport drinks, rounding up stray cups, or handing out fruit.

Jim Cotter, a physician at the Napa offices of Kaiser Permanente and a member of the marathon board, likes to relate his initial experiences staffing the aid station at 22 miles. "All week long," he observed, "we're dealing with patients who are not well, who are seeing us because something is wrong with them, and they are cranky and out of sorts. It sometimes seems as though you can't do enough to make

them happy. Then you come out here and you hand a cup of water to a really healthy runner at 22 miles, and they react as though you've just told them they won the lottery. 'Oh, thank you, thank you,' they go on, just for giving them a cup of water. Our medical volunteers love it. They feel really needed and appreciated."

Many runners have such reactions to the volunteers. In 2001 the weather was cold and wet and windy, and we received numerous e-mails after the race complimenting a Boy Scout troop that staffed one of the aid stations. "It was cold and windy and wet and here were these Boy Scouts, standing out in the rain, handing us Gatorade while they were shivering, and they were telling us to have a good race. They were wonderful," one of the e-mails gushed.

There is a very real feeling of fulfillment that comes from serving as a volunteer. There is also a wonderful feeling of camaraderie among volunteers who are working as a team, and the feeling of community—ironically—is strengthened even more when the volunteers survive a particularly trying day, whether working in bad weather or handling unanticipated numbers of runners.

A great deal of satisfaction can result from helping people achieve their goals, from being a part of their accomplishment—even if it involves merely handing them cups of water.

And the sense of camaraderie with other volunteers can't be beat. The volunteers at the Western States 100 Red Star aid station come from all over the state of California, and for most of them, it is the one time a year they see each other. Over the 20-plus years we've staffed it, we've seen volunteers' kids grow into adulthood, get married, have their own kids, and bring their kids along to be part of the Red Star family. Volunteers leave Red Star with smiles on their faces from a job well done and a "See ya next year!" on their lips.

For Your Consideration

- Why not sit down with your yearlong racing schedule and come up with a formula that would allow you to volunteer for perhaps every 5th race you do, or every 6th; even every 10th would be a big help toward keeping the sport alive.

- Pick one race a year that might grow on you as a volunteer opportunity, and turn it into an annual rite of whatever season it is; then lure several of your friends to come along and help out.

- Also, pick one race a year in your area and double up by volunteering to help out in advance of race weekend and also racing it. In a way, you would be tripling up, because as a racer on the course,

you could take note of places where the race could be improved from the racer's perspective.

- If you have the opportunity to coach or train newbie runners, incorporate the concept of volunteering into your coaching or training.
- If you are considering moving up to ultras, consider volunteering to work as a pacer for other racers so that you can gradually get your feet wet in the sport. In the process, you will be helping other runners achieve their goals.

SPECTATE

Long-distance racing is not one of the more interesting sports to spectate, unless you briefly study a race—especially a megarace—as pure human spectacle. But even then, you see the runners file past and disappear, and then you turn around and go home. It's not like a 10,000-meter race at a track where the runners circle 24 times and you can literally see the whole thing from the stands. Track races reveal textbook strategies such as runners who do not have particularly good kick picking up the pace midway through the race and wearing down the runners who rely on a kick at the end to win.

Road races, unless they run on a loop course, are difficult to watch; your little microcosm is way too limited and over way too fast. Of course, the occasional course lends itself to leap-frogging to various points along the way. The 2007 U.S. Men's Olympic Marathon Trials in Central Park and the women's Trials the day before the Boston Marathon in April of 2008 were such examples. If you were willing to hoof it across Central Park or between Boylston Street and Commonwealth Avenue, you could see the best marathoners go by within 10 feet (3 m) of you 8 to 10 times. It was a spectator's heaven.

In one of my editorials in *Marathon & Beyond,* I proposed that directors of road races consider holding them at automobile road racing courses, such as the 1.99-mile (3.2 km) course at Sears Point, Sonoma County, California. The hilly, winding course would be challenging but dramatic, and all the necessary infrastructure is right there, everything from toilets to concession stands, grandstands, and adequate parking to the pits, where runners could grab their sport drinks. A marathon (the Marathon de Sears) would involve just a bit more than 13 circuits of the course. Because of the hills, there would be no world records, but it would be plenty fun. Families and friends could spread out picnic lunches on the grassy areas where currently, in late June each year, NASCAR fans spread out tablecloths covered with fried chicken and beer. Spectating at such a facility would be luxurious.

Of course, most of my ideas fall flat. It's been roughly 10 years since I proposed that one, and nobody anywhere in the world has followed up on it. So in the meantime, literally hundreds of perfectly good automobile road courses throughout the world muddle through occasional fallow weekends where the only action is the janitor watching the grass grow.

Spectating a road race is not necessarily easy and often is not overly rewarding. However, when you are the one running a race, there's no feeling like the one you have when you come upon a knot of spectators who've taken up a place along the course to cheer you on.

Some races are replete with spectators. The Boston Marathon course is lined with spectators; the nicer the weather, the more spectators there

are, some years as many as a million. The runners love Boston not so much for the course as for the support they receive along the entire 26.2 miles from a sporting public that is famous for loving its sports and knowing who's who, even if there happen to be 25,000 whos running in the same race.

New York City, of course, is similar. I recall the first time I ran the New York City Marathon, back in 1978. As I ran through Harlem, a wizened old African American man with few teeth left stood along the curb handing out orange slices from his own homemade aid station. As I went by, I waved off his orange slice. "If I was you, young white boy, I'd run a little faster," he said. Of course, he was only joking. Well, at least he was smiling when he said it. He was one of the only spectators out on the streets of Harlem that day, and 30 years later I still remember him and appreciate his taking the time to cheer us on . . . and to urge us to run a little faster.

On the opposite end of the mass-spectator road race are my memories of the old Humboldt Redwoods Marathon course near Weott in far Northern California. Back in the 1980s, the course wasn't a double out-and-back as it is today. It was a single out-and-back that ran from the Dyersville Bridge down the one-and-a-half-lane asphalt road through the redwood forests to Miranda and back. One of the last years I ran it, they had added a half-marathon that started at the same time. Unfortunately for us marathoners, just before Myers Flat, the half-marathoners turned back while we kept going. It was one of the eeriest feelings I've ever had in a marathon: One minute I was running along with hundreds of people, and a minute later I was all alone with my breathing, my foot plants, and the towering redwoods, and not another human being in sight. In some ways it was disconcerting because it happened so quickly, but in other ways it was refreshing, because I was alone with the redwoods as my audience, silently inspiring me to go on.

Of course, you can have every intention of being a good and enthusiastic spectator, only to find that you've been drafted into a different role. When I started college in September of 1964 in central Pennsylvania, I saw on the announcement board at the lounge that there was going to be a cross-country meet at 10 a.m. on Saturday. Most students went home over the weekend, and the campus was usually pretty quiet and empty, a perfect time to work on book reports and term papers.

On Saturday morning, I wandered on up to the edge of the campus after consulting the map of the course and stood huddled down inside my winter coat as the winds howled in from Canada. It was too cold to take my hands out of my pockets to consult my watch to see how close I was to the start of the race. Suddenly, an old battered '62 Rambler Classic came chattering clattering up to me, a purple cloud of burning

motor oil trailing it. A blonde crew cut fellow with buck teeth jumped out and asked if I was there for the cross-country meet. When I said I was, he hustled me into the passenger seat of his car and we roared up the road. He stopped at an intersection, handed me a red flag, and told me to stand there. When the runners came toward me from campus, he explained, I was to wave the red flag in the direction of I-80; but when they came back, I should wave the flag toward the steep downhill road that intersected the main road. He was off with a clanging protest from his engine, and I was standing beside a lonely road as snow began to fall.

Sure enough, eventually a pack of runners came toward me expelling frosted breath like a herd of desert mustangs. I pointed out toward I-80, and in a rush of that steaming breath, they were past. I turned and waited, and sure enough, eventually a strung-out gaggle of runners came toward me from the direction of I-80 and I directed them down the steep hill. Then they were gone. I stood there waiting, the red flag squeezed between my upper arm and the side of my chest, my frozen hands stuffed down inside my pockets. And I waited. The snow fell and the wind tried to quick-freeze my shivering body. I had just decided to walk back to campus when the battered Rambler appeared and Coach Brady gave me a ride back to my dorm. (I think he came back to get his red flag; I just happened to be attached to it.)

The next week I joined the team, figuring it was easier to run and stay warm than to stand around freezing as the only spectator the cross-country team had that day. The old adage that we also serve who only stand and wait didn't hold much meaning for me that day.

But I still remember vividly my first and last day as a cross-country spectator.

Slightly better conditions (but not by much) greeted us spectators in Central Park on November 3, 2007; we had come to watch the U.S. Men's Olympic Marathon Trials. The course involved five laps within the park, so if we stayed stationary, we could see the field go past five times. If we didn't mind jogging across the park, we could catch the field an amazing 10 times. It was one of the most inspiring races I'd ever watched. We could get so close to the runners that if it had been a warmer day, we'd have been sprinkled with marathoner sweat. As it was, we collected a half-dozen special drink bottles that competitors tossed to the fans. Again, it is a race that, as a spectator, I'll remember for as many years as my brain keeps working.

A spectator at the right place at the right time can make the race for a runner who needs a little pick-me-up at that point. A cheer from the sidelines, no matter how feeble, does not go unheeded by passing runners. To be noticed and acknowledged for trying to do your best makes the accomplishment all the sweeter.

When a local race comes up and you aren't going to run in it, take the time to cheer on those who are competing; it will help make their day special. And, passing good things forward, maybe at your next race there will be at least one additional spectator out there cheering you on.

But if you see a ratty old Rambler lumbering toward you before the race starts, run the other way.

For Your Consideration

- On race days, when you aren't competing, consider attending as a cheering spectator; you might be surprised to find that you feel almost as good as the runners you cheered on.

- Pick a race each year to use as a spectator party; get your friends together and pick a prime spot along the course and turn it into an annual event.

- Check the schedule for your local high school cross-country home meets, get some friends together, and go out and cheer the team on. Most high school cross-country teams don't have a very large following, and they greatly appreciate any sort of support on race day.

- If you haven't been a spectator at one of the famous megaraces (the New York City Marathon, Spokane's Lilac Bloomsday Run, Atlanta's Peachtree Road Race), you might be surprised at how much fun it is to line the course with tens of thousands of other fans and cheer on the leaders, the middle-of-the-packers, and the rear-enders.

- If a friend of yours is going to do her first road race, make a point of going out to the course with a sign to cheer her on. Don't tell her in advance, though; you'll be delighted at how thrilled she will be to see you there.

STUDY RUNNERS AND RUNNING

with

Roger Robinson

In running, as in most areas of human endeavor, we latecomers plod forward in the footprints of the giants who preceded us. Every discipline, every area of interest has its own unique history, its antecedents. And so it is with running, arguably the oldest sport and lifestyle on earth.

It is always fascinating in the world of popular music to see the next hugely hyped band come careening down the pike. The band's praises are sung to the stratosphere, millions of kids go ga-ga for their records (sorry . . . CDs), and in a year's time they are barely a footnote in a thousand-page encyclopedia of pop rock. But while they are here, they are invariably compared to the Beatles, the implication being that because they are newer than the Beatles, they are better. Of course, they never are (better, that is), and sometimes even their "newer" doesn't play well against a 437th listening of "Norwegian Wood." Fortunately for the evolution of good taste, in every generation that comes along, several million kids discover the Beatles for themselves and make them popular all over again—to the outrageous extent that, as chapter is written, the Beatles' collection of number one hits (titled, simply, *1*), made it on the list of best-selling albums (sorry . . . CD) of all time.

The kids defy the market and the marketers by gravitating toward better music—in this case the originals, not the pretenders. (Oh, yes, The Pretenders; but that's a whole other group.) In the process, they more fully enjoy the music because they more thoroughly understand from whence it came. After all, the Beatles had their influences, too, mostly rhythm and blues and rockabilly music.

The same phenomenon does not seem to be occurring with long-distance running. There are millions of runners these days, but most of them affect a glazed-over look when you mention Frank Shorter, much less Emil Zatopek, Ernst van Aaken, Clarence DeMar, Roberta Gibbs, Frank Zuna, Tom Osler, Edward Payson Weston, and Pheidippides. (Yes, long before pop music stars such as Cher, Madonna, Prince, and Bono made single monikers chic, there was ultrarunner Pheidippides—and that was 2,500 years ago.)

Many runners these days have no more idea in whose footprints they run than they have of the major export of Chile or the capital of South Dakota. (By the way, it's copper and Pierre, respectively.) Just as significantly, they have little knowledge of what the depletion phase of carbohydrate loading is, what fartlek training is, or in some cases, how long a marathon is.

As an aside, I'm involved with the Napa Valley Marathon, and not too long ago we received a desperate/irate e-mail from a woman who demanded to know how long our marathon is. She had gone to a half-dozen marathon Web sites, and none of them revealed just how long their marathons are. That's our second-favorite query; our first came four

times one year when, after the race, we received four e-mails wanting to know what the hell we were doing starting the race on time.

Back in the 1970s, such questions would have been unthinkable. New runners were mentored by grizzled veterans, they read voraciously about the stars of running and tirelessly researched training programs, and they often socialized after a race, exchanging pertinent information, comparing notes, and egging each other on to greater efforts the following weekend.

Today much of what long-distance runners grasp as knowledge and information comes off the Internet, and much of that is either useless or just plain wrong. Roughly a year ago we were asked by a book publisher to review a manuscript about running that they were considering publishing. We didn't have to go very far to form an opinion. On the first manuscript page, there were four grievous errors of fact.

This is not to imply that there are people bumping around the running world who know everything. However, a good number of people who have been around a few decades and are still available do know quite a bit about the subject of running in all its wonderfully varied manifestations.

I don't want to imply that everyone who runs needs to become a running encyclopedia. After all, a driver who couldn't even begin to explain how an internal combustion engine works can still manage to drive a car. And knowing how an internal combustion engine works doesn't guarantee that the person is an excellent driver, although it might help. NASCAR driver Dale Earnhardt Jr. and Indy car owner Roger Penske have at least an inkling of what a carburetor and a crankshaft do.

In anything we do in life, we derive more profound and thorough enjoyment from it if we know something about it. Attend a performance of Richard Wagner's opera *Ring of the Nibelung* without knowing who Wagner was and what a nibelung is, and you'll get awfully confused by all the shouting and gesticulating and finger pointing and spear brandishing. But read up on Wagner and on Norse legends and read some of the libretto in English, and your experience will be greatly enhanced.

So too with running.

Runners remain some of the most voracious readers on the planet. Demographically, they are surfing on the crest of modern technology, but they also love the written word and frequently love to discuss every aspect of a book until it is thoroughly understood and absorbed. Ask a group of five experienced runners what the best running novel of all time is, and you'll get five different opinions and a good hour of lively discussion. If you ask them what the best training program is, once again you'll have initiated a heated discussion on the merits of Higdon versus Henderson versus Daniels versus Lydiard.

The upside of the Internet is that it makes it incredibly easy to access book-search sites. What used to be a chore (going to a bookstore and filling out forms and waiting for two weeks for a book) can now be done almost instantaneously online. And for the more popular of the classic running books, the prices are lower than the cost of shipping them.

There is a philosophy that you should take time to know your enemies if you are to avoid or defeat them. In a reverse philosophy, you should take time to know your friends (in this case, the writers, coaches, and teachers who have gone before or are still available) so that you can have the maximum help they can provide to improve your overall experience of the running life.

I am reluctant to list here Web sites that occasionally or often include running history items or stories because often Web sites vanish into the ozone with sprintlike rapidity. (I list some sites in online appendix C, which you can view at http://tinyurl.com/35g17mg. Especially good is www.joehenderson.com, where Joe makes available much of the writing about running he has produced over the past five decades, including some complete books.)

Being old-fashioned and the Luddite that I am (I'm writing the first draft of this on a Royal standard typewriter), I tend to get a lot of information—especially historical information—from books and magazines, which is why this chapter is so print-friendly.

Most of the Web sites of the regional and national running magazines contain some history, as do Web sites for most of the longer-running races. The Web site of the Boston Athletic Association, www.baa.org, contains accounts of every Boston Marathon from the first one, way back in 1897.

Additionally, check with your local running club and running stores; they often bring in guest speakers who cover some interesting aspect of the history of running and are an excellent resource. Often, with the slightest urging, members will spin tales of the days of yore.

Also, make an effort to catch Dick Beardsley when he speaks at a race; some of his stories of naivete when he started running in the 1970s are hilarious. And Wikipedia, for its several shortcomings, is fairly reliable if you feed in the names of famous runners or renowned races.

One of my favorite running writers is Roger Robinson, who frequently writes articles on the history of running for *Running Times* and *Marathon & Beyond*. I asked him how his passion for reading about running developed. This is his reply; he titles it "History and Heroes: Why Study Running?":

> *The first running prize I ever won, in a high school cross-country meet, was a faded copy of the Jubilee History of the International Cross-Country Union, published in 1953. It was old-fashioned hard-back, full*

of dry year-by-year race narratives and results, and it gave the names of all the officials in big type. (They produced the book.) Blurry black-and-white photos showed teams standing formally in a line in baggy tracksuits and little mustached Frenchmen and Belgians racing for their lives in muddy shorts.

That book changed my life. It opened up for me a heroic history, a story that had enriched the century and laid the foundation of a global sport. (The old "International" was the forerunner of today's World Cross-Country Championship.) It showed me that running was not just games at school; it had a great international tradition. Although I was not a specially gifted teenage runner, I felt that I might be a small part of that tradition.

That sense of belonging in the history of running and adding to its significance enriched every race and every training run for me for more than 50 years. When, incredibly, I was actually selected some years for the World Cross-Country, it was as if that old book were coming to life—I almost wished our tracksuits were baggier. When I ran my first marathon, I sensed the footsteps of the heroes I had read about—Spiridon Louis, Dorando Pietri, Emil Zatopek. Finishing Boston for the first time, my head was full of Clarence DeMar, the John Kelleys, Dave McKenzie, Kathrine Switzer.

The more I read and learned, the more enjoyable and worthwhile running became. It doesn't add up to much if you do it only for yourself, but it's richly rewarding when you understand how every run contributes to something bigger.

Many good runners are experts. A boy runner living near me in Wellington, New Zealand, used to spend hours watching videos of Jack Lovelock, Peter Snell, and John Walker, and reading about New Zealand's running tradition. Now Nick Willis has added to it, winning the Olympic 1,500-meter silver medal. Any young Kenyan will recite that country's running roll of honor for you.

That's why now I write about running, especially its history. If I can give other runners the inspiration of knowing the full meaning of what they do, I will have repaid the faded book that opened the window on history for me in the late 1950s.

For Your Consideration

- Check out the list of 25 Running Books You Should Read in online appendix B (http://tinyurl.com/35g17mg), and then visit the Internet book-search sites and begin pulling together a little running library. Most of the books in paperback cost only a few cents, especially if they were best-sellers in their time.

- Set aside some time each week for an hour or so of reading up on the history of the sport, profiles and biographies of the great runners, and how-to books on improving your running.

- If you belong to a running club, why not suggest forming a book club of a half-dozen or a dozen fellow runners; bouncing ideas around about what the book is saying often opens up new insights and a more profound understanding of the sport and lifestyle.

- Don't overlook the ready availability of videos of various running movies, from *Running on the Sun* (an ambitiously produced look at the grueling Badwater 135 ultramarathon and the crazy people who attempt it each year) to *On the Edge* (the takeoff, starring real-life runner Bruce Dern, of the famed Dipsea Race in Northern California). The Web site www.zombierunner.com has a terrific selection at good prices.

- Keep current with the new crop of running books. We are in the middle of another resurgence of books about running: everything from biographies of famous runners to personal accounts of running feats to how-to and training volumes. Read to run better. In my case, it keeps me from having to steal hubcaps to stay solvent.

TEACH OTHERS
TO RUN

Running is one of the simplest of all physical activities—an activity that largely accounts for our existence today (thanks to our fleet-of-foot ancestors). As one of running's pundits once said: "Running is so simple just about anyone can do it; all you do is put one foot in front of the other and then alternate." Done regularly, long-distance running bestows its own arsenal of physical, psychological, and spiritual benefits.

Only relatively recently have we come to ignore our physical side. And we can all see the disastrous results of ridding our society of physical activity: obesity, diabetes, high blood pressure, several forms of cancer associated with obesity (colon, endometrial, and postmenopausal breast cancer; *Newsweek*, March 7, 2008, p. 12), depression, back injuries, and so on.

It is startling to look at 50-year-old newsreels. There are virtually no obese people. Children are all playing physically active games . . . outside. And this isn't Depression Era years we're talking about; this is the post–World War II era. People worked physically challenging jobs. Children played actively, had physical education classes at school, and went outside to run around during recess.

Today many children are what used to be referred to as bumps on a log. They do virtually nothing physical, and their diets are atrocious. In many cases they learn their deathstyle from their parents. We are seeing the first generation of people in the United States who will likely die younger than their parents did.

All it takes to turn things around is a bit of regular exercise—and I'm not talking about exercising the fingers on a computer keyboard or texting messages on a smartphone (the logical outcome of that will be carpal tunnel syndrome).

Do we have a health crisis in the United States? We sure do, and it isn't confined to a lot of people sitting around without health insurance. Probably 85 percent of the health problems Americans have are self-induced, what I like to call diseases of choice. Most of them can be traced back to a sedentary deathstyle complicated by a deadly diet.

Some years ago I had the pleasure of coauthoring five books with Elaine LaLanne, the charming wife of perennial fitness guru Jack LaLanne. I asked Jack if it was more important to good health to engage regularly in physical fitness activities or to have a healthy diet. Without missing a beat, he pointed to the former. "A regular fitness regimen covers a whole host of sins," he said. As he heads toward the 100-year-old mark, his real-life learned wisdom has been borne out repeatedly. Let's look at a few 21st-century headlines about exercise:

> "Clearing Confusion About Exercise: Member of Committee That Wrote New Guidelines Says Less Than an Hour May be OK," *Washington Post*, February 15, 2005.

"Feds: Eat Smarter and Exercise More," Marilyn C. Preston column, *Tribune* Media Services, January 27, 2005.

"New Federal Diet Tip: A Lot More Exercise," *New York Times*, January 13, 2005.

"Harder Workouts May Pay Off," *New York Times*, June 12, 2007.

In case you believe that none of the preceding applies to you, your anatomy and genes say otherwise: "Human Race Has Marathon Ancestors: Scientists Conclude Modern Anatomy Shaped by Need to Run Long Distances," by Robert Lee Hotz, *Los Angeles Times*, November 18, 2004.

I'm not going to bore you with a whole chapter on what's wrong with the typical American lifestyle. It's pretty obvious. And people know what the solution to the problem is. At the conclusion of literally every study on the subject, the recommendations are more exercise and better dietary habits. What I *am* going to do is propose something that will not turn the problem around overnight, but rather, something that could double what is right with a segment of America.

According to Running USA (www.runningusa.org), the nonprofit organization that brings together under one umbrella various aspects of the running movement (shoe manufacturers, race directors, promotional companies, some of the media), there are currently 11,583,000 runners in the United States, if you define a runner as someone who ties up the ole shoelaces and goes out the door for a run at least 100 times in a year. (More casual runners, defined as those who run at least six times a year, number 29,246,000.)

This number includes people who run on a semiserious basis at the low end of the spectrum to people at the other end of the spectrum who run hundred-mile races, as well as those elite athletes who regularly train more than 120 miles (193 km) a week.

Our local marathon, the Napa Valley Marathon (a member of Running USA) is sponsored by Kaiser Permanente, the largest health care maintenance company in the United States. One of the factors that sets Kaiser apart from other health care organizations is that it spends a lot of time working to prevent sickness and disease rather than merely treating it once it raises its ugly head. Its Thrive program pushes members to take an active role in their own health by promoting physical fitness and positive lifestyle choices.

Dr. Jim Cotter, himself a marathoner and a member of the board of directors of the Napa Valley Marathon, made some welcoming remarks before the 2008 race to the assembled runners. "If Kaiser had a membership that was as active and healthy as you are, all we'd need to do is sit around reading magazines all day."

Dr. Cotter's point is a good one. Wishing and hoping for good health just doesn't cut it. Complaining about poor health just doesn't cut it, especially when for most of us there are obvious ways to turn it around on our own.

An enormous amount of good could be accomplished by instigating a modest running program. Running is simple. It is relatively inexpensive: an old T-shirt, a pair of shorts, and a decent pair of shoes and you're off.

Did you know that studies reveal that in most families of regular runners, most of the other family members don't run? Pretty startling. But that statistic also sets up a very wonderful place to start turning some of the negative lifestyles of Americans around. Think of the health impact if every American runner got one other American to run! The numbers are staggering. The changes in the country's sickness and disease rates in one year would be monumental.

Consider that it takes roughly two months to get into good enough shape to run comfortably on a regular basis. Consider that the most impressive fitness gains come to those who are new to the sport. Consider that most of the illnesses Americans suffer from are self-inflicted and can be "cured" with regular exercise. Each person lured into running would attain better health than a medicine chest full of drugs could offer.

Running lowers body weight. It firms muscles and skin. It lowers blood pressure. It delays and often heads off osteoporosis. Running has frequently been used by people who have wanted to rid themselves of addictions. (It has, in fact, been called a positive addiction.) And, running has been studied as a means of combating depression. "A number of preliminary studies have shown that aerobic running produces significant improvement in the condition of moderately depressed clients," wrote Gary W. Buffone in *Running as Therapy* (Sachs & Buffone, 1997, p. 6). A regular running program provides a virtual cornucopia of health benefits, both physical and psychological.

But, you might say, I'm not a coach. I wouldn't know what to do to help someone run.

As a coach, all you need to do is pass along what you know about the subject. Running isn't all that complicated. We already made the point that it is one of the most basic of human activities. If you have been running any decent length of time, you've obviously picked up the basics, and probably some of the finer points, as well.

Why not share your lifestyle with someone in your life who is important to you? It is an excellent opportunity to have a positive effect on that person's life. It is also an opportunity to make special memories by running and racing together. (Of course, do be aware that you may be creating a monster. Your friend or family member may end up being

a faster, better runner than you are. If so, so much the better. You can take all the credit for creating a champion.)

There is great satisfaction in teaching through coaching, especially if it is a subject about which you are passionate. Joe Henderson, one of running's most noted writers on the sport and lifestyle of running (and editor of *Runner's World* from 1970 to 1977), took up the coaching of runners several years ago in Eugene, Oregon. I've known Joe for decades and have always been impressed with his dedication to writing about running; but his passion for coaching people to become runners (or marathoners) far outshines his love of writing . . . something I never thought I would see.

The same can be said of my brother Drew, who has been coaching high school cross-country for years. Some of his most satisfying days over the past two decades came from seeing the positive changes in some of the kids he coached. But that's not all. Over those two decades he has amassed a small army of graduated members of his team who have become his friends. Drew is frequently invited to the weddings of his former runners. Sometimes they invite him to get-togethers in out-of-the-way places (one gathering of a dozen of his former runners was in Colorado; he lives in eastern Pennsylvania). They stay in touch, sharing their postschool lives with Drew and with each other.

Following the lives of his former runners has been invigorating for Drew. He has been especially pleased to see how the discipline they learned to run long distances well translated to other aspects of their lives. Coaching has added an uplifting aspect to his life.

Both Joe Henderson and my brother Drew would be the first to admit that they probably get much more out of the process of coaching than their runners do.

You don't need to be a genius about running to be a good coach. You need only study the sport, be open to picking up trends, see and record the results of your efforts, and be empathetic. All of this is within the realm of those who have been in the sport for even a limited amount of time.

Every once in a while a coach can have a profound impact on a person's life. His passion for running can be transferred to one of the people he is coaching, sometimes in the process turning that person's life around. It's happened for Joe and for Drew.

Giving back to the sport by taking on coaching duties can be very fulfilling. You can improve a friend or loved one's life while improving the overall health of these United States.

The phrase "Put me in, Coach" will take on a whole new meaning.

For Your Consideration

- The United States is in a health crisis.
- Running is a very proactive solution.
- You are a person who runs and who knows about running.
- Pick out a person in your life whom you cherish but who is not yet a runner. Become a running mentor and coach to that person.

START OVER

People typically stop running for one of two reasons: they become injured, or they burn out (which is a form of mental and sometimes spiritual injury).

Most physical injuries can be turned around with a combination of medical treatment (formal or home-grown) and rest. Rest can also play a major role in bringing a runner back from the darkness of burnout. Several notable world records in running have been set in the wake of a world-class athlete being forced by injury to endure a rest period he or she would not have taken voluntarily. (Derek Clayton did this twice in the 1960s, coming off a forced layoff to set world records. Joan Benoit-Samuelson did it in 1984, winning the Olympic gold medal. Meb Keflezighi did it in 2009: coming off a recovery from leg injuries that observers believed would end his career, he won the New York City Marathon.)

But perhaps as important as rest is taking a break from the whole world of running, which amounts to giving the spring an opportunity to refill and refresh its cooling waters.

In considering this concept of a well or spring that needs refilling, the age-hewn take on it from veterans of the running wars is this: The physical well (that is, the well that needs refilling due to some physical ailment) is the easiest of the three to refill. Next, and more difficult to replenish, is the psychological well. The most difficult of all to refill is the spiritual well—a well that runs deep and takes a whole lotta cooling liquid to refill. (I discuss this in chapter 6, Eschew Racing.)

Most "serious" (i.e., obsessive) runners do not have the patience to wait for a physical injury to turn around. Some long-distance runners who have earned stress fractures by overdoing it have been put in casts by their podiatrists only to saw off the cast when they couldn't manage to wait the six weeks until the bone healed. Of course, being that kind of a patient from hell usually has a single outcome: repeated injury and a lot more time off from running than would have been the case if he or she had followed doctors' orders.

Some see such action as heroic and to be emulated. They rationalize that those obsessive types love their running so much that they can't do without it. This can't-do-without-it is often the attitude of someone who came to running to use it as a positive addiction to get control of a negative addiction, such as substance abuse. What it is, of course, is a weakness, an inability (or unwillingness) to control themselves. In the long run, it does them no good—no good for their beleaguered bodies, and no good for the sport and lifestyle of running in general.

If you spend perfectly good money and time to go to a qualified sports medicine specialist and then insist on ignoring everything the specialist tells you to do to get better, well, what can I say? Good luck. Consider suing yourself when the healing fails to take hold.

Psychological burnout is a different matter, although in some instances it can be related to physical injury. If, as an example, you repeatedly reinjure yourself because you come back too soon, eventually you are going to become psychologically bummed, which of course will negatively affect even the remaining good aspects of your running, such as the good friends you've made through the sport.

Psychological burnout doesn't need to be linked intimately with physical injury. It can just as easily be caused by overracing, piling on too much mileage too soon, or overextending a running season so the body gets no time to catch its breath. This latter condition is often common in areas of the world where the weather is conducive to training and racing all year long.

Simply put, too much running or racing with too little programmed easy time can burn you out to the point where you can no longer stand the thought of training and racing again. Your body needs an easy season at least once a year to allow all the minute muscle tears to heal and for the head to avoid mental vapor lock.

Some very accomplished runners (ultrarunner Marshall Ulrich and gold medal marathoner Joan Benoit-Samuelson, for example) look forward to the first snowfall to shift from beating up their legs to schussing along the cross-country ski trails.

When you burn yourself out psychologically, you will find that you need to force yourself out the door to get in a scheduled run. When you burn yourself out spiritually, you can't even find the lock to open the door. You can't even force yourself to think of running. There is no longer a spiritual connection between you and the lifestyle of running. The spiritual aspect of running goes far beyond the physical act of running. It infuses all aspects of your life. When it goes, there is a huge black hole in the center of your life. A terrible darkness descends that cannot be dispelled by the most beautiful of days.

It sounds like treason to say this, but when the joy of running has left you hollow and empty, the best thing you can do is go with the feeling. Give it up, at least for the time being. Make a deal with yourself that you will abandon the lifestyle of running, which, you must admit, seems to have abandoned *you*! Set a decent period of time during which you do not run, do not think about running, do not obsess about it, just plain ignore it. Be generous with yourself. Remember the depth and the breadth of that spiritual well. Give yourself a year.

It sounds like a long time, a very long time, but if you want to return to running refreshed on all levels, you need to allow the well to refill. You need to respect your own needs— on all levels.

I'm infamous for using automobile analogies when discussing running. I'm going to shock all my Luddite buddies by using a computer

analogy this time. Almost once a month I give my computer a command to print something and it won't do it. It won't even warn me that it isn't going to cooperate. It's as though the link between the computer and the printer has vanished. I assume it has something to do with the printer software in the computer getting screwed up or getting short-circuited. What do I do to restore harmony between the computer and the printer? Maybe you're not supposed to do this, but I instruct the computer to restart itself. It turns off, turns back on, and Voila!, the connection between the computer and the printer is restored. The same can be applied to a running program. Stop it. Restart it. It's refreshed, and so are you.

What do you do after the year without running ends? Start from scratch. Be a rank beginner, because that's what your body is going to want you to be. Your body is going to want to be gentled back into the sport, then gradually into the lifestyle. To be precipitous is to chance a renewal of the injury merry-go-round or to restart you on the road to excess once again.

Your patience of waiting a year has allowed literally every little muscle tear and connecting tissue bruise to heal. There is no such thing as a born-again virgin; it's physically impossible. But it is possible to be a born-again running virgin, one with some hard-won wisdom from a previous life in running.

Take your time, enjoy the process, don't expect too much too soon. This time around, correct all the mistakes and blind alleys you encountered on your original foray into running. And reset your goals to the realistic levels your years of experience in running have taught you are possible.

Reject impatience. Set goals to compete at different distances than you specialized in the last time around. Run more miles simply for the joy of moving rather than for putting mileage in your log. If you weren't a member of a running club before, join one. Volunteer at races. Lure a friend into the lifestyle, someone you think would benefit from it on several levels.

Give yourself a break, and don't demand too much too soon. Your body will let you know when it's ready for the climb to the next level, as will your mind and your spirit.

Baby yourself at first. Wallow in the new running you. Certainly it is very cliche, but pause and smell the flowers. Judiciously used, running can extend your life on every level. Listen to the gentle bellows of your breath, feel the coursing of the blood through your veins, explore the opening of your mind to simpler things, and be an animal worthy of the body you inhabit.

For Your Consideration

- If you suffer an injury, give it more rather than less time to heal.

- If you're going to pay a medical professional good money to diagnose your injury and offer advice toward recovery, take the advice you paid for.

- If you are psychologically burned out, give yourself permission to back off or stop completely.

- If your burnout reaches such depths that your spiritual side is involved, make a major commitment to give the spiritual well plenty of time to refill.

- Consider giving yourself a year off so that you can start over fresh, doing everything right this time.

Glossary

Every specialized area has its own nomenclature, or lexicon. Consider the electronics industry. In the last half-century it has coined words and phrases from *blog* to *e-mail blast* (in fact, *e-mail* itself), *gigabyte* to *pixel*.

Most of the terms used in the long-distance running world have an origin in the greater language; they've just been a bit expanded, bent, or reimagined. Here are 25 terms every runner should know to communicate with other runners. Actually, there are more than 25, because there are so many instances of two terms for one thing (e.g., *bonk* and *hitting the wall*). Besides, I've never been good at math.

acclimatization—The customization of the human body for a variety of jobs. One's body can over time be trained to run either in unusual heat by gradually exposing it to additional loads of heat or at a higher-than-normal altitude by gradually building up its volume of work at altitude.

aerobic—A physiological term referring to a condition "with oxygen"; that is, the exercising body is performing at a level at which it is receiving enough oxygen to continue at its current pace. Once the exercising body picks up speed or workload, it can quickly pass the anaerobic threshold. See *anaerobic*.

anaerobic—A condition ("without oxygen") during which the exercising body has advanced past its capacity to receive enough oxygen to continue at its current pace. Once the anaerobic threshold (also called the lactate threshold) is passed, the exercising body's time to continue moving at that pace is severely limited by physiology.

bib—The number pinned to a runner's chest to identify him or her to the scoring personnel at a race. (Old-fashioned runners still refer to it simply as a "number.")

biomechanics—In running, the mechanics of how one moves over the ground. It is how the various systems of the human body work with each other to facilitate movement.

blood doping—A controversial method of increasing the oxygen-carrying capacity of the blood by removing blood from a runner's body, storing it, and having it reintroduced into the body before a

competition where it theoretically increases red blood cell count and hence the oxygen-carrying capacity of the body.

bonk—A term originally used in bicycling to indicate the point at which the body has used up its available energy to supply the working muscles. Runners still frequently refer to this phenomenon as hitting the wall. See also *hitting the wall.*

carbohydrate loading—This should actually be called carbohydrate overloading. In preparation for a marathon or a long run, the runner cuts back on the intake of proteins and fats and concentrates on loading up on carbohydrates, which serve the exercising body as fuel. (The old and dreadful practice of entering a depletion phase and depleting carbs to wring the sponge dry before overloading the body with carbs late in the process has pretty much been done away with because merely increasing carbs has been shown to work just as well.)

chafing—The discomfort produced when body parts rub together or clothes rub body parts without the benefit of lubrication during the process of running.

chondromalacia—The wearing away of cartilage under the kneecap, which produces pain while running; also known as runner's knee.

chute—The corridor (often consisting of brightly colored ribbons) leading away from the finish line in a race.

cross-training—The use of other aerobic sports (cross-country skiing, pool running, bicycling) to supplement but not replace running as a means of increasing long-distance running fitness. Cross-training, of course, is used constantly by triathletes.

DNF—An acronym for "did not finish."

ekiden [Pronounced ECK-uh-din.]—A Japanese word for a marathon relay usually in the following format: three 5Ks, two 10Ks, and a 7.2K. The event traces its roots to a Japanese version of the American Pony Express: Runners passed along a written message until it reached its destination.

fartlek—A Swedish word meaning "speed-play." In running, fartlek is a method of increasing leg speed by periodically (during a longer run) picking up the pace. Typically, a runner does the increase in speed between preestablished points along the course or arbitrary points established along the way (e.g., "Let's pick it up at the next telephone pole and hold it for four poles").

gels—Gel pockets inserted into the soles of running shoes; introduced in the 1980s by Asics in response to Nike's air pockets.

glycogen—The fuel of choice for endurance athletes. Because the body contains only so much glycogen, after several hours of activity, one must consume carbohydrates to replace used glycogen stores. See also *carbohydrate loading* and *bonk.*

hard/easy training—Alternating hard sessions (doing speed workouts at a track, racing shorter distances, or doing long, sustained runs) with easy sessions so that the body can recuperate and thereby come back stronger for the next hard session.

hitting the wall—Reaching the point during a marathon or ultra at which one's body has depleted its stores of electrolytes (about two hours of which are stored in the muscles and liver). This phenomenon can be avoided by taking in electrolytes (e.g., from sport drinks) during the run.

interval—The rest period between repeats of a set distance, usually one-half lap or a full lap, but among more serious runners as little as 200 meters or one-quarter lap. This term is often mistakenly used to indicate a set of repeats of a set distance at a track workout in which one does repeat laps at a faster-than-usual leg speed. What the runner is actually doing is repeats (see *repeats*).

jog—A synonym for slow running and a word despised by "real" runners. As times in races slow, however, the term is coming back into favor.

kilometer—A measurement in the metric system equal to roughly two-thirds of a mile.

LSD—An acronym for "long, slow distance"; refers to long runs done at a steady pace slower than race pace. The term is often credited to Joe Henderson, who wrote a book on the subject in 1969. The term actually originated from coaches Arthur Newton, Arthur Lydiard, and Ernst van Aaken, and has been misinterpreted over the years to mean running long distances at very slow speeds.

marathon—A footrace of 26 miles, 385 yards. Also, a town in Greece; previously a plain on which a small Greek army repelled a much larger force of invading Persians in the year 490 BC. Legend has it that a Greek hemerodromi ("all-day runner") named Pheidippides (see also *Pheidippides*) carried a message of the Greek victory to the capital of Athens (a distance of roughly 24 miles) where he announced "Nike!" ("Victory!") and dropped dead. The now-standard marathon distance was first run at the 1908 Olympic Games in England; the longer marathon distance was used to give the royal family a better view of the race both at the start and at the finish inside the stadium. The now-standard distance only gradually came into its own. The Boston Marathon, as an example, used the 26 mile, 385 yard distance from 1924 to 1952; then reverted to a 25-mile, 938-yard distance from 1953 to 1956 before reverting to the standard distance in 1957. *Marathon* also refers to any event that lasts a long time (e.g., a marathon dance contest, a marathon negotiating session).

negative split—A race in which the runner runs the second half faster than the first half. (Everyone talks about doing this, but few do.)

orthotics—Custom-made shoe inserts, usually prescribed by podiatrists. Orthotics are intended to compensate for the oversights of nature and the abuse heaped on feet, legs, and even the lower back by runners.

overuse injuries—Injuries caused by running too much, too early, and too often. Running too often in the same way stresses body parts repeatedly until they fail.

pacing—A method of rationing out one's energies over the full distance of a race course to reap maximum results.

peaking—The art and science of bringing one's training to a peak at the right moment to achieve the best possible performance at a specific event.

personal record (PR) or personal best (PB)—One's own best performance at a given distance (i.e., competing against oneself). The term PR is used primarily in the United States; PB is used in most other places around the world.

Pheidippides—Often—and wrongly—referred to as the Greek messenger who ran from the Plains of Marathon to the gates of Athens to announce the Greek victory over the invading Persians, only to then drop dead. Actually, the legend of Pheidippides dropping dead after delivering his message was stitched together centuries after the battle. The proto-historian Herodotus cited Pheidippides as the all-day runner the Greeks sent to Sparta to ask for military help. Sparta was 150 miles away. Because of religious beliefs, the Spartans could not send help at that time, and Pheidippides ran back 150 miles to report that the Spartans would not be coming in time to help. A Greek all-day runner who would fall and die after a mere 24 miles would have been an embarrassment to his profession. See also *marathon*.

relay—A long-distance event in which a team of runners takes turns running segments of the course; can also refer to team races on the track in which multiple runners take turns running legs of an event, such as a mile relay in which four runners each run one lap of a track.

repeat—A term primarily used when referring to a track workout in which the runner repeats at a brisk pace a preset distance, usually involving one, two, three, or four laps of the track. The runner walks or jogs a set interval between the repeats of the set distance, usually a half-lap or a full lap. See *interval*.

ultramarathon—Typically, anything longer than a marathon, but generally considered to begin at 50K (31 miles). There is no upper limit.

warm-up—A preparatory activity to warm up the muscles before running; typically involves jogging (to loosen running muscles), stretching (to loosen various muscle groups), and strides (short bursts of fast running) to wake up muscles for the work to come. The shorter the event, the more the runner needs to warm up.

25 Pertinent Quotes

I wish chiefly to impress on all athletes who may read this book that if they wish to excel at any branch of sport they must train. Train steadily, consistently, and constantly, and always bear in mind that however well they may be doing it is possible for them to do better.

Alf Shrubb, one of the greatest of English long-distance runners of the first half of the 20th century

The long run is what puts the tiger in the cat.

Billy Squires, famed coach of runners such as Bill Rodgers, Alberto Salazar, and Dick Beardsley

A lot of people don't realize that about 98% of the running I put in is anything but glamorous: 2% joyful participation, 98% dedication! It's a tough formula. Getting out in the forest in the biting cold and the flattening heat, and putting in kilometer after kilometer.

Rob de Castella, famed Australian long-distance runner

The marathon begins at 20 miles.

Frank Shorter, 1972 Olympic marathon gold medalist

Second place is not a defeat. It is a stimulation to get better. It makes you even more determined.

Carlos Lopes of Portugal who, at 37 years of age, won the Olympic marathon in Los Angeles in 1984

We are different, in essence, from other men. If you want to win something, run 100 meters. If you want to experience something, run a marathon.

Emil Zatopek, the greatest distance runner of his era

The marathon can humble you.

> *Bill Rodgers, four-time winner of the*
> *Boston and New York Marathons*

I have never been a killer. I'm not an aggressive personality and if I can remember any emotion I felt during a race it was fear. The greatest stimulator of my running was fear.

> *Herb Elliott, perhaps the greatest miler of all time;*
> *he never lost a mile race in his life*

The long distance runner plods on mile after mile, day after day, week after month after year. People turn to stare, and children who have a legitimate reason for being in the park without a golf club in hand want to know why I'm running.

> *Hal Higdon, in his classic book,*
> On the Run From Dogs and People

The secret of my abundant health is that whenever the impulse to exercise comes over me I lie down until it passes away.

> *J.N. McEvoy, 1938*

A colleague reported that a patient of his, a competitive runner, often ran against the flow of runners during workouts because when running behind men he felt an uncomfortable impulse to stare at their buttocks. Running against the flow, he experienced pleasure at feeling that people would admire his strong and graceful stride and might even notice the bulge of his genitals in his skimpy briefs.

> *Michael Sachs, PhD, "A Psychoanalytic*
> *Perspective on Running,"* Running as Therapy

Running is like going to a spring: each of us drinks our fill, and new runners come, pushing aside those in front.

> *Michael Sandrock,* Running With the Legends

I learned years ago when I was training about 24 kilometers a day that if I shifted the daily balance to 32 kilometers one day and 16 the next, I got better reactions without increasing the total distance I was running.

> *Arthur Lydiard, famed running coach*

Where do you dwell when you are running?

> *Joshu Sasaki Roshi, Japanese Zen teacher*

You cut your journey as much from your own personality as you do from the external world around you, so no one can say much that will help you understand what it means to meet your small and large self during the commitment to forward motion that will continue day after day through your waking hours. From the moment you begin until the moment you finish you are committed to an indivisible problem whose only solution is constant and unrelenting effort.

Jim Shapiro, Meditations From the Breakdown Lane: Running Across America, *as he began his journey at the Pacific Ocean in California*

[Running] gives a sense of free movement and personal physical power. If we race, it gives the excitement, risk, reward and drama of competition. It can give the rich companionship of running with friends, or the equally rich solitude of running alone. It gives the joy of learning the textures of the earth with your feet, and the fulfillment of taking your body beyond its known limits. In origin it is associated with escaping danger and succeeding in the hunt, both essential to life. It is so simple, so pure, so enjoyable, so rewarding, and yet so arduous. Nothing matches a hard run in what the poet Yeats called "the fascination of what's difficult."

Roger Robinson, Running in Literature

Epilepsy, paraplegia, blindness, deafness—what do these unfortunate afflictions have to do with running, which is surely a pursuit of the immensely fit? Simply that some men and women bearing these burdens are active, enthusiastic, and sometimes quite formidable runners. This is all part of a remarkable situation: people with a large spectrum of handicaps—from temporary neurosis to lifetime disability—have found running not only possible, but also an acceptable way to return to the unafflicted world; to be like, or even better than, the "ordinary person," to experience those heady sensations, traditionally denied to the handicapped—victory, or even hard-conceded defeat.

Dr. Peter Wood, Run to Health

Without a race every so often, I lose the sense of awe at what I can do when I press myself, and at the same time I know my humility. I forget that racing can make the impossible possible and the possible impossible. Only here can I end up running faster than I ever thought I could or unable to cover a distance I've gone a thousand times before.

Every race is a question, and I never know until the last yards what the answer will be. That's the lure of racing.

Joe Henderson, The Long Run Solution

There is more to failing than picking yourself up out of the dust, brushing off the grime and trudging onward. For every defeat, there is a victory inside waiting to be let out if the runner can get past feeling sorry for himself.

Ron Daws, The Self-Made Olympian

In autumn, the sound of my belch is heard through the land. Fall is the Camelot of runners. There are races everywhere—races run in air turned crisp and invigorating, the perfect temperature for distance running.

But the races also bring tension. In those minutes before the start, I feel threatened. I know I may be beaten. I know I will surely feel pain. And not only my mind knows this, my entire body knows it and acts accordingly. Hence, the belch. That is the way I react when I am in a situation where I am embarrassed, frustrated or apprehensive. The belch is something rarely uttered in anger. It is not the roar of a lion, but the bleat of a sheep.

Dr. George A. Sheehan, Dr. Sheehan on Running

A male runner in distress is a heroic figure; a woman runner in distress is further proof that we are fragile creatures who are physiologically unsuited to marathon running.

Kathrine Switzer, Marathon Woman

The goal I can neither reach nor let go of is out there somewhere. I dread meeting it. So until it shows its face I will continue to do what I have always done. I will keep on doing my best.

Joan Benoit-Samuelson, Running Tide

Running myself to the point where I stagger or am totally drained is not heroic, but a poor show of misused energy. I will retire from the race long before I reach such a state.

Tom Osler, Ultra-Marathoning

I do believe that the [Boston] marathon is bigger than its sponsors and bigger than its creator, the Boston Athletic Association—so much so that if no one put up the money and the BAA could not manage the race, runners would still gather at the Hopkinton town green to run to Boston on Patriots' Day. If the towns refused to issue permits to allow the race to pass, I believe runners would risk arrest to run.

Tom Derderian, Boston Marathon

Running is a way of life for me, just like brushing my teeth. If I don't run for a few days, I feel as if something's been stolen from me. I look forward to my runs. I run alone. I don't like to wait for people. It's a great way to get acquainted with yourself. I love it. I just go along and think the good thoughts, think about my life. The air is fresh and sweet.

Johnny A. Kelley, two-time Boston Marathon winner
and three-time Olympic marathoner;
completed 58 Bostons in his lifetime

Bibliography

Annerino, John, *Running Wild: An Extraordinary Adventure of the Human Spirit*, Thunder Mouth Press, 1992, 1998, 317 pp.

Benoit, Joan with Sally Baker, *Running Tide*, Knopf, 1987, 213 pp.

Benyo, Rich, *The Exercise Fix,* Human Kinetics, 1989, 145 pp.

Benyo, Richard, *Making the Marathon Your Event*, Random House, 1992, 365 pp.

Benyo, Richard, *Return to Running*, World Publications, 1978, 235 pp.

Benyo, Richard, *Running Past 50*, Human Kinetics, 1998, 242 pp.

Bowerman, Bill J. and W. E. Harris, M.D., *Jogging: A Medically Approved Fitness Program for All Ages*, Grosset & Dunlap, 1967, 127 pp.

Brant, John, *Duel in the Sun*, Rodale, 2006, 210 pp.

Burfoot, Amby, editor, *Runner's World Complete Book of Running,* Rodale, 1977, 306 pp.

California Track & Running News, January/Febuary 2008, 36 pp.

Campbell, Joseph and Bill Myers, *The Power of Myth,* Anchor, 1991, 293 pp.

Chodes, John, *Corbitt*, TAFNews, 1978, 154 pp.

Clayton, Derek, *Running to the Top*, Anderson World, 1980, 137 pp.

Cooper, Dr. Kenneth H., *Running Without Fear*, Bantam Books, 1985, 257 pp.

Costill, David and Scott Trappe, *Running: The Athlete Within*, Cooper Publishing, 2002, 191 pp.

Csikszentmihalyi, Mihaly, *Flow: The Psychology of Optimal Experience*, Harper & Row, 1990, 305 pp.

Daniels, Jack, *Daniels' Running Formula*, Human Kinetics, 2005, 287 pp.

Daws, Ron, *The Self-Made Olympian*, World Publications, 1977, 158 pp.

DeMar, Clarence, *Marathon*, New England Press, 1981, 156 pp.

Derderian, Tom, *Boston Marathon*, Human Kinetics, 1994, 1996, 635 pp.

Galloway, Jeff, *Marathon!*, Phidippides Publication, 1996, 199 pp.

Glasser, William, *Positive Addiction*, Harper Collins, 1976, 176 pp.

Harper's Magazine, June 2007, 13 pp.

Henderson, Joe, *Long Slow Distance: The Humane Way to Train*, TAFNews, 1969, 62 pp.

Henderson, Joe, *Run Right Now: What a Half-Century on the Run Has Taught*, Barnes & Noble, 2004, 336 pp.

Herodotus, *Histories,* Oxford University Press, 2008, 240 pp.

Higdon, Hal, *Marathon*, Rodale, 1993, 207 pp.

Jerome, John, *The Sweet Spot in Time*, Summit, 1980, 349 pp.

Karnazes, Dean, *Ultra-Marathon Man: Confessions of an All-Night Runner*, Tarcher, 2005, 280 pp.

Karp, Jason, "Chasing Pheidippides," *Marathon & Beyond,* May/June 41 pp.

Lydiard, Arthur, *Arthur Lydiard's Running Training Schedules*, Track & Field News, 1970, 20 pp.

More, Daisy and John Bowman, *Empires: Their Rise and Fall: Aegean Rivals: The Persians, Imperial Greece,* Boston Publishing Company, 1986, 174 pp.

New Oxford American Dictionary, 3rd ed.

Newsweek, March 2008, 12 pp.

Parker, John L., Jr., *The Frank Shorter Story,* Runner's World Books, 1972, 47 pp.

Reese, Paul with Joe Henderson, *Go East Old Man,* Keokee, 1997, 273 pp.

Remy, Mark, *The Runner's Rule Book: Everything a Runner Needs to Know— and Then Some,* Rodale, 2009, 166 pp.

Robinson, Roger, *Running in Literature: A Guide for Scholars, Readers, Runners,* Joggers, and Dreamers, Breakaway Books, 2003, 304 pp.

Sachs, Michael L. & Buffone, Gary W., editors, *Running as Therapy: An Integrated Approach,* Jason Aronson, Inc., (1984) 1997, 341 pp.

Sandrock, Michael, *Running With the Legends: Training and Racing Insights from 21 Great Runners,* Human Kinetics, 1996, 592 pp.

Sheehan, George, *Dr. Sheehan on Running,* World Publications, 1975, 205 pp.

Shorter, Frank with Neil Amdur, *Diet Pepsi Guide to Running,* PepsiCo., 1978, 90 pp.

Sillitoe, Alan, *The Loneliness of the Long-Distance Runner,* Signet, 1959, 144 pp.

Squires, Bill with Raymone Krise, *Improving Your Running,* Stephen Greene Press, 1982, 206 pp.

Switzer, Kathrine, *Marathon Woman,* DaCapo, 2007, 418 pp.

Ward, Michael, *Ellison "Tarzan" Brown,* McFarland & Company, 2006, 443 pp.

Wood, Peter D., D.Sc., Ph.D., *Run to Health,* Charter Books, 1980, 351 pp.

About the Author

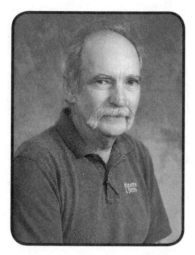

Richard Benyo is a longtime runner who over the past 30-some years has competed in distance races from 400 meters to ultramarathons and has completed 37 marathons. Named Journalist of the Year by the Road Runners Club of America, he is the former executive editor of *Runner's World Magazine* and Anderson World Books, Inc., and is currently the editor of *Marathon & Beyond* magazine. He has written 22 books on running, health, and fitness, including *Running Past 50* and *Running Encyclopedia*.

Benyo was inducted into Running USA's Hall of Champions in 2005, and he currently resides in Forestville, California, where he enjoys sailing when he is not running or writing.

About the Contributors

Dick Beardsley has a terrific story to tell, and he tells it extremely well. A talented runner in college and beyond, Dick rose to fame primarily as a marathoner. He holds a record for improving his best marathon time 13 consecutive times, starting with his first-ever marathon. He is perhaps best known, however, as one-half of the famed "duel in the sun" duo with Alberto Salazar, where, on a hot day in Boston 1982, the two waged a furious battle for the entire 26.2 miles, Beardsley finishing a mere two seconds (2:08:51 vs. 2:08:53) behind Salazar. But the high point had not yet

arrived in Dick's life, and that high point came as his lowest point. His leg nearly amputated in a farming accident, Dick underwent numerous operations, only to suffer additional accidents until surgeries and hospital stays became routine. In the process, he became hooked on prescription drugs, and began a downward spiral that ended with his being caught forging prescriptions. After a horrendous recovery, Dick gradually returned to running—and began speaking of his experiences. He quickly gained a reputation as one of the best motivational speakers on the circuit. Today he continues to speak and inspire and heads the Dick Beardsley Foundation.

Joan Benoit-Samuelson will long be remembered as the gutsy runner who ran away with the gold at the first-ever women's Olympic Marathon in Los Angeles in 1984. Coming off knee surgery a mere 17 days before she won the U.S. Olympic Marathon Trials, she completely dominated the Olympic event. When the pace seemed too slow for her, she made the audacious move to run away from the pack and looked over her shoulder to find that none of her competitors was coming with her. Joan had burst onto the marathon scene five years previous when she entered the 1979 Boston Marathon wearing a Bowdoin College shirt and a Boston Red Sox cap backward and ran a 2:35:15, slicing a massive eight minutes off the course record; she came back to Boston in 1983 and ran an astonishing 2:22:43, a then-world record. Not to be pigeonholed as merely a fierce runner, she is also a race director, heading up the very popular Beach to Beacon 10K in her native Maine. In addition, she is a master gardener.

Amby Burfoot won the 1968 Boston Marathon, following in the footsteps of his mentor, John J. Kelley, who won a decade before; following in Amby's footsteps was Bill Rodgers, his college roommate at Wesleyan, who won Boston four times. Amby has been associated with *Runner's World* since 1978, when he was hired as East Coast editor; since then he has served as executive editor and more recently as editor at large. One of Amby's New Year's Day traditions is taking a dip in the nearest ocean. On Thanksgiving

Day he runs the Manchester (CT) 5-Mile Road Race, which he has been doing for more than four decades. Amby is also the author of several books on running; his best is *The Runner's World Guide to the Meaning of Life*.

Joe Henderson has written 27 books on running and countless magazine articles. He authors the "Joe's Journal" column for *Marathon & Beyond* and was for more than 30 years a columnist and editor at *Runner's World*. A veteran of more than 700 races, Joe teaches running classes at the University of Oregon in Eugene and coaches a local marathon team. His most classic running book is *The Long Run Solution*; he jokes that he has written only one book, but he's rewritten it 27 times. He lives in Eugene, Oregon, famous for its running legends.

Hal Higdon is the author of 35 books, including a novel about the 72 hours leading up to a major marathon. It is titled simply *Marathon*. Hal's best-selling nonfiction book is the similarly titled *Marathon: The Ultimate Training Guide*. Between his books and training programs (available on halhigdon.com), Hal probably has trained more than a half-million runners to do 26 miles 385 yards.

Dean Karnazes was named one of the top 100 most influential people in the world by *Time Magazine* several years ago; *Men's Fitness* hailed him as one of the fittest men on the planet. He is also one of the most creative ultrarunners in the world, constantly cooking up unique first-time challenges. In 2008 he ran 50 marathons in all 50 U.S. states on 50 consecutive days. For 10 years, he's run the 200-mile Relay from Calistoga to Santa Cruz, California, not as part of one of the 12-person teams, but solo. He's run

across Death Valley in 120-degree temps and he's run a marathon at the South Pole in minus 40 degrees. He is the author of the bestseller *Ultramarathon Man* and has appeared on dozens of television shows, most notably a classic appearance on *The David Letterman Show* in the wake of his attempt to run 300 miles without sleeping.

Deena Kastor was the first American woman to break the 2:20 barrier in the marathon and continues to be the American record holder in that event. She won the bronze medal in the marathon at the Athens Olympic Games in 2004. She is a three-time Olympic athlete: Sydney, Athens, and Beijing. She was the winner of the 2005 Chicago Marathon and the 2006 London Marathon. She holds the American record in the 5K, 8K, 12K, 15K, 20K, half-marathon, 25K, 30K, and 35K. Over her career she won 24 national championship titles. Her other great passions are cooking, entertaining, and eating. "What a great balance of energy consumed and energy used," she says. She is also a voracious reader, "so I can't wait to have *Timeless Running Wisdom* as my couch companion."

Lorraine Moller competed competitively on the track and on the roads for more than 20 years. Representing her native New Zealand, she competed in the Olympic Women's Marathon the first four times it was contested, winning the bronze medal in 1992 in Barcelona. She also competed at various distances in the Commonwealth Games, winning the bronze in both the 1500 m and 3000 m in 1982 (Brisbane) and silver in the marathon in 1986 (Edinburgh). She ran her first marathon in 1979

at Grandma's Marathon (Duluth, Minnesota) in 2:37:37, sixth-fastest time by a woman at that time. She commenced to win her next seven marathons. She won the Avon Women's Marathon three times (1979, 1982, 1984) and won Boston in 1984. She is currently a coach, author, and motivational speaker; she lives in Boulder, Colorado.

Roger Robinson for many years led a double life as a senior academic (now emeritus professor) at Victoria University, New Zealand, and as an elite international runner representing England and New Zealand and setting masters records at the Boston and New York City marathons. He brought his scholarly and sporting interests together in books like *Running in Literature* and *26.2 Marathon Stories* (coauthored with Kathrine Switzer, his wife) and in many of his articles on the past and present of running. He won the George Sheehan Award in 2006 and the RRCA Journalism Excellence Award in 2009. Selected writings are available on www.roger-robinson.com.

Bill Rodgers, born and raised in Connecticut, is known to serious road racers as "Boston Billy" Rodgers for his domination of the famed Boston Marathon (which he won four times, the first time—in 1975—in an American record time). He moved to Boston and has been an institution there for decades, where he trains while running the Bill Rodgers Running Center in the North Market Building of the famed Faneuil Hall Marketplace. During one period at the height of his career, he won 22 road races in a row, everything from the 10K to the marathon, earning him the nickname of King of the Roads. Although there has always been a serious competition between Boston and New York City, Boston Billy dominated marathons in both cities, winning the New York City Marathon four times. He is the author of *Marathoning* (1980) with legendary Boston newpaperman Joe Concannon. Billy continues to run and race and work as an ambassador of the sport of long-distance running.

Allan Steinfeld worked closely with Fred Lebow to make the New York City Marathon the most famous big-city marathon in the 1970s by bringing it out of Central Park and onto the streets of the five boroughs of New York City; he came onboard in 1986 as technical director. When LeBow died of brain cancer, Allan rose to president of the New York Road Runners Club; in 1994 he became the chief executive officer of the NYRRC and race director of the NYC Marathon. He early on established a reputation as one of the nation's leading authorities on the technical aspects of road racing. He was also instrumental in establishing and fostering several associations overseeing the sport of running, including the Association of International Marathons (where he served as vice-president) and Running USA (where he served for years as president). He served as chief referee of both the men's and women's Olympic marathons in LA in 1984. He is a member of the Distance Running Hall of Fame.

Kathrine Switzer was the first woman to wear bib numbers and officially run the Boston Marathon, incurring the rage of the race codirector who attacked her midstride and tried to throw her out of the race. The event changed women's running history and inspired Kathrine to go on to run 36 marathons, win the 1974 New York City Marathon, and become the founder and director of the Avon International Running Circuit where she organized 400 races in 27 countries for over a million women. Switzer used these events to help secure the women's marathon event into the Olympic Games. She is now an Emmy award–winning TV commentator

of marathons as well as the author of *Marathon Woman* (her memoir) and *Running and Walking for Women Over 40* and coauthor with husband Roger Robinson of *26.2 Marathon Stories*. She still runs regularly and although she doesn't take competition seriously, she lets no woman with gray hair pass her in the finishing straight.

Marshall Ulrich is one of those all-around (or renaissance) kind of guys, especially when it comes to ultra-feats. He has achieved the triple crown of extreme sports: world-class ultrarunner, Seven Summits mountaineer, and record-setting adventure racer. Among his feats: He reached the summit of the highest peak on all seven continents (and did it on the first

attempt in all seven instances); completed all nine Eco-Challenge adventure races; crossed Death Valley a record 21 times, including a solo and a 586-mile quad crossing; completed a 3063-mile run across America in 52.5 days breaking the masters and grand masters record; won the Badwater 146 four times; completed the Leadville Trail 100 and the Pikes Peak Marathon on the same weekend; and completed all 100-mile trail races in 1989 finishing in the top 10 in five of them. "Marsh" holds a BA in fine arts from University of Northern Colorado and for 25 years ran a successful business. Over the years he has raised more than $800,000 for charities.

Mel Williams, PhD, FACSM, is an eminent scholar emeritus at Old Dominion University in Norfolk, where he taught exercise physiology and sport nutrition over the course of 40 years. His major research focus has been performance-enhancing aids in sport and he has published numerous books on the subject, which have been translated into 10 languages. He is committed to maintaining a high level of personal fitness for both health and sport competition and has completed more than 100 marathons and ultramarathons, including all Marine Corps Marathons and the Kona Ironman Triathlon.